Chrysalis

A journey into the new spiritual America

by Mark Allen

PAN PUBLISHING
P.O. BOX 4416
BERKELEY, CALIF.
94704

Cover by Lorena Laforest Bass
Full-page artwork by Rainbow Canyon
Artwork on tops of pages by Dean Campbell
Cover photo by Michael Bass

Copyright © 1978 Mark Allen Donicht

Special thanks to Shakti Gawain and Franz Ross for their support, encouragement, and assistance.

*Typeset in 10 point Palatino at
Another Point, Oakland, California*

First Edition

Library of Congress Cataloging in Publication Data

Donicht, Mark Allen.
  Chrysalis, "a journey into the new spiritual America".

  1. United States—Religion—1946-   2. Spiritual life.
3. Donicht, Mark Allen. 4. Religion—Biography. I. Title.
BL2530.U6D66   291.9   77-28335
ISBN 0-89496-011-3

This book is dedicated to a lot of the people who shared something special with me in this journey... Dedicated with love and appreciation to:

My parents, Anne and William Donicht, Sr.
My brother, Will Donicht
Tom Olson
Carol Swardson
Lulu Spurgeon
Tony Steblay
Linda Kelsey
Arthur Ballet
Robert Tembeck
Prof. Arya
The Beatles
John Donahue
Eddie Felien
Syd Walter
Nancy Walter
Marlow Hotchkiss
Danny Campbell
Gwynneth Swardson
Charlie Swardson
Nina Hotchkiss
Lily Hotchkiss
Surya Singer
Daniel Moore
Laura Allen
Katsuki Sekida
Star Atherton
Jeremy
Gino Scandler
Barbara Neill
Mildred Jackson
Walt Whitman
Elvis Presley
every poor poet
Mary

Franny
Dick Draper
Ray Chapeau
Becka Donicht
Kathy Dieter
Suzuki Roshi
Tarthang Tulku, Rinpoche
Chogyam Trungpa, Rinpoche
Paul Clemens
Randy Prieser
Ken Keyes, Jr.
Kent Nerburn
Shakti Gawain
Jon Bernoff
Kimberly Wilcox-Horne
Summer Raven
Robert Powell
Jim Gleason
Claudia Ray
Susan Madley
Buckie Zahner
Bobbin Zahner
Peter Dupont
Dean Campbell
Ruth Roberts
Patrick Roberts
Nanette Holt
Steve Stottlemeyer
Julie Stottlemeyer
Ruthie Schwarz
Dave Foxworthy
John Ney
Holly Franzen
Ralph Steiner

John Lilly
Monica Wheeler
Tolly Burkan
Jesse Phillips
Rainbow Canyon
Michael Bass
Lorena Laforest Bass
Chiuh Gawain
Collin Wilcox
Michael Wilcox-Horne
Buffy St. Marie
Jeanie Greene
William Blake
Janice Cohen
Jim Hurtak
Jay Franklin
Egon Merz
Israel Regardie
Catherine Ponder
Kathryn Kuhlman
Gina Merz
Patricia Sun
Indira Tara Deva
& every lover I've ever known
Buddha
Padma Sambhava
Shiva
Tara
and
Jesus
and
Mu
and
Sara
and
you

Contents

Part I — Days of Darkness

A glance back	9
The Firehouse Theater	13
Heavy days	25
A crack in the shell	31
Yoga	32

Part II — Days of Light

Theater of Light	42
Zen	64
Maui	80
Gypsy life — Northern California	83
Creative Anarchy — Southern Oregon	88
Pilgrimage to San Francisco	95
Altamont	101
Chogyam Trungpa, Rinpoche	106
Suzuki Roshi	108
Tarthang Tulku	109
Lama	111
Tibetan Buddhism	117
American Tantra	126
Miracles	138
Going home	141
Magic	142
Living Love	144
Silva Mind Control	148
Relationship	150
Kaskafayet	152
Making Love	154
Now. . .	159
A Dream, a Reality	165

Appendix
    The study of psychology: East and West   169

Suggested Reading   177

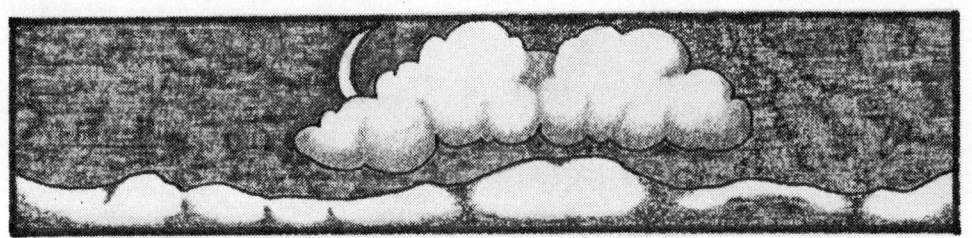

A journey into the new spiritual America. . .

Near the end of my college years, it seemed as if something of deep importance was missing . . . something intangible, unnamable, but deeply felt.

I sometimes had the vague feeling that maybe my father, or my teachers, had known something which they hadn't told me which would in some way make sense out of the whole empty and confusing system of American life. . .

I started college in 1964, a Freshman at the University of Minnesota. I felt that my first two years there were very fine, generally — it was a time of growth, of creative interaction with many very alive, even brilliant people. . .

But later, in my Junior and Senior years, '67 and '68, I became very disappointed, disillusioned with the University — and even more deeply, with life in general.

Looking back, I can see this time of confusion as a blessing — for it is in this confusion and frustration and vague despair that the real fruitful search for meaning, for wisdom, begins. . .

This is the story of my search . . . and my discovery. . . Perhaps I can share some of it with you. . .

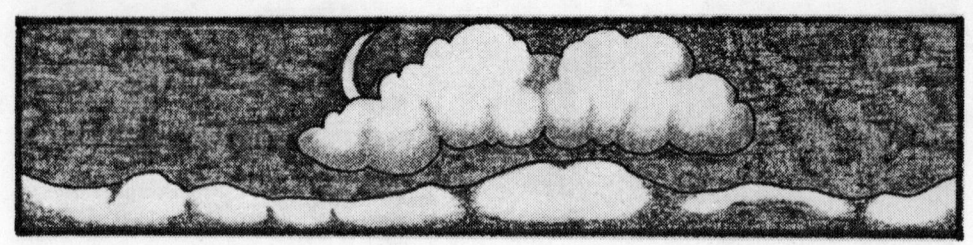

A note regarding the form of this book:

Sideheads

I've used sideheads to give the reader a quick glimpse of what's happening on each page. This makes it easier to roam through the book and find the parts that are most relevant and interesting to you, if you like.

Feel free to skip around in it, to wander thru it in no particular order. The sideheads will be a guide, generally, to what's happening.

A note about the dots:

... and dots

I use dots or periods in an unusual way. . .

Most people read too fast, I feel — we're taught how to read rapidly, but we usually haven't been taught how to read in depth. . .

When you come to the dots, *slow down*. . . maybe even take a breath. . . Take a moment to absorb it.

A glance back

UNTIL THE MID-60s, I — like so many others — had maintained an illusion that all was well with the world... In high school, I had bought into the game of achievement, and I had excelled — though of course there were those that were far better, as there always are... It was naturally assumed that I would go to college, and I went, without question.

I began college in 1964 with the same values I had when I left high school. The only difference was that I was living on my own...

My first year of college began very much like high school, in most ways... Things were changing all around me, but I was not really aware of it, yet, on a conscious level...

An event called the "Vietnam teach-in" happened during my first year of college... There was a *war* going on, although we were constantly being told it wasn't a war, it was something else, a *military conflict*, to which we were sending *military advisors*, in large quantities, for the government was drafting heavily... The University presented a large symposium, with many speakers and many different points of view...

I walked into that 'teach-in' as a kid from the suburbs who didn't really know what was going on in that conflict, and I walked out committed in my heart to bringing a swift end to it in any way possible. It was a radicalizing experience for many, many young people. The pro-war people seemed *unreal* — incredibly cold and distant, talking about economics and military advisors, talking like would-be Nixons, in a strangely unbelievable way, like poor actors... And the anti-war people seemed so warm and loving and humanitarian... including Norman Thomas, who was 90 years old at the time, and who won over the crowd, effortlessly, with his gentleness and humor and wisdom...

The times were changing, rapidly — and yet everywhere, especially in the mass media, people were intent upon denying that any change was occurring... It wasn't until the

Memories of high school

First year of college:

'Vietnam teach-in'

a radicalizing experience

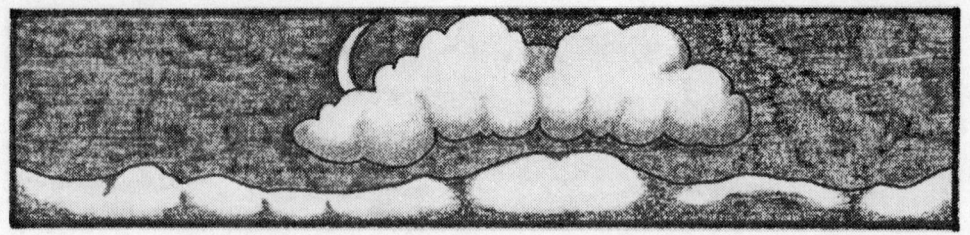

70s that the mass media admitted that deep change had taken place in the 60s...

Second year of college: deep change

In my second year of college, the changes started happening very rapidly, on very different levels, simultaneously... First, we discovered grass... and then acid... and widespread change seemed to be happening instantly...

I remember smoking grass for the first time... listening to the Jefferson Airplane's first album. Music had never sounded so rich, so lush, so filled with something that was the very essence of life... filled with wonder...

I remember walking thru Minneapolis, late at night, stoned, seeing everything with new eyes, and thinking, "This grass has shown me something: I'm going to have to *change*..." It was as if I had the choice to change deeply, or to leave the most progressive thinking and lifestyles alone and to continue in the life I was leading...

I leapt at the chance to change... I had been growing more and more discontent with the life I was leading... It all seemed so ego-oriented — designed for personal satisfaction, and very little more... It all seemed so empty... Existentialism reigned...

and basic questions

I began to examine everything in a new light... I began to question deeply the whole system of education I had been spoonfed since childhood... Why the emphasis on grades — on personal achievement compared to someone else's personal achievement? Was it really necessary?

And why is the emphasis on doing so much so quickly? To take an average credit load, you had three to five courses, each of which would demand a great amount of study and work and writing...

In order to do very well, you had to read very fast, with very little time to absorb anything, to reflect — to deepen, in meaningful ways. You had to *cram*... That's what we called it, and that's what it was...

My last two years of college got very strange — surreal, at times — darkly Existential, absurdist... The reality which I created for myself was heavily influenced by people with names like Camus, Samuel Beckett, Harold Pinter, Ionesco, Sartre... I was a Theater Major, and we were very influenced by these people — they spoke so passionately, so deeply — they were the epitome of Western philosophy, going beyond all others before them... Life was *Waiting for Godot*... You were a *Stranger*... a *Rebel*, a cosmic joke... God was dead to the hearts of many...

My last two years of college: darkly Existential

We wove a web of encapsulation around ourselves. At the time, it was painful, uncomfortable... Later on I saw that web of darkness as a cocoon, a chrysalis — a time of darkness just before the dawn of a new life...

T HE WAR in Vietnam was getting absurd. The news media would keep announcing that it was not a war, and then we would see live, instant newsreels of the action — as hot as any Marvel Comics or old war movies — and we'd hear the fatalities reported, usually sounding something like, "400 Communists were killed, and there were 20 American casualties..."

The war was getting absurd

The underground papers were screaming that most of those 'enemy casualties' were women and children... But no one was believing the underground papers...

Things were getting very strange... Not too many wars had an organization formed of veterans who were *against* it...

I told my father, in a rare visit home those days, that if I was drafted, I wouldn't go. He looked at me with the most intense expression I'd ever seen on his face... He slammed his fist on the table that was between us, containing yet expressing more anger than I'd ever seen in him before...

and so was my father

His words were classic — I remember them well. He looked me in the eyes and said: "Your grandfather went in. Your father went in. Your brothers went in. *You'll* go in!"

I couldn't believe it. To me, it was the height of absurdity — it was the stupidest logic I had ever heard.

I looked at him and laughed, and said no more. There was nothing my father could say or do to change my mind. And

11

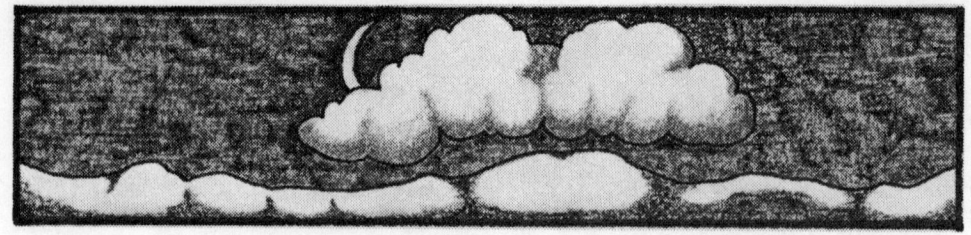

there was nothing I could say or do to change his. . . So I said nothing. . . For the next several years, there was very little communication between me and my folks — or between me and the whole straight world, in fact. . . It seemed that the existential philosopher Camus was right: I was a stranger. . .

Changes: leaving school,

A rapid series of events led to a change. . . I met a lady named Carol, and I had a chance to join a so-called 'radical' theater company called The Firehouse Theater. It would mean leaving school. It would mean facing the draft, too. But I left school, without a second thought. And I didn't look back.

meeting Carol

THE FIRST TIME I ever saw Carol Swardson was in a little Japanese restaurant in Dinkytown, Minnesota — right near the University campus. . .

She fulfilled all the models I had at that time of an ideal lover: she was classically beautiful, with long red hair, a small, exquisite body, a face which looked like it was sculpted by a very loving creator (which it was!). . . And she was intelligent, outspoken, with a bright sense of humor and joy of living. . . She was very strong, and commanded her own space in a way that really impressed me. . .

I felt magnetically drawn to her. . . I somehow sensed she had a lot to teach me. . . And she was so beautiful. . .

I found out later that she was 10 years older than me — she was 31, and I was 21 — and she had two kids. . . It made it all the more intriguing. . . But she was involved in a pretty solid relationship with a man named Marlow Hotchkiss, one of the directors of the Firehouse Theater. . . Yet, in my dreams, in my fantasies, I put it out there: somehow, someday I wanted a deep relationship with that lady. . .

Little did I know that it would all come true, and in a very short time. . .

The Firehouse Theater

I HAD HEARD a great deal about the Firehouse Theater in Minneapolis, but had never seen them until a writer named Mike Steele took me to one of their rehearsals. It was late in the year of 1967 — I was a Senior at the University. I was instantly and deeply impressed by the atmosphere of the work: the intensity, the intellectual depth, the freedom, the group energy, the open physical contact, the honest encounters between people. . .

I went back, saw them do *Peer Gynt* — which was wildly explosive — and then *Happy Days*, which was beautifully and painfully done, conveying the dark and absurd and ironic view of existence of all of Samuel Beckett's work. . .

Then, during their next play, *Jack Jack* by Megan Terry, there was an opening for someone who could play the piano. . . I've been playing piano since I was 10 years old, so I joined, as a musician and an actor. It was an awakening for me — a rebirth — a rediscovery of theater as a meaningful tool of investigation and expression and growth.

Jack Jack was a loud and clear and exuberant expression of hip culture rebelling against the corporate giant culture (a recurring theme of my life at that point). The play was about freedom and honest exploration and individual rights and nudity . . . and it was about *me* — and Carol and Marlow and Syd and all the rest of the troupe, because everything the Firehouse performed came from a totally personal center; the work was almost always autobiographical in so many ways. . .

The life of the Firehouse was intense, constantly changing, open and honest. All of its directors and leaders have impressive minds — highly creative, each in a different kind of way. Yet it was Carol who impressed me most deeply.

Carol is intelligent, outspoken, often even almost brash in her open communication with people. She was a deeply radical influence in the company — at first, politically, and

Seeing the Firehouse Theater

and joining: an awakening

Carol: a radical, a visionary, a beauty

13

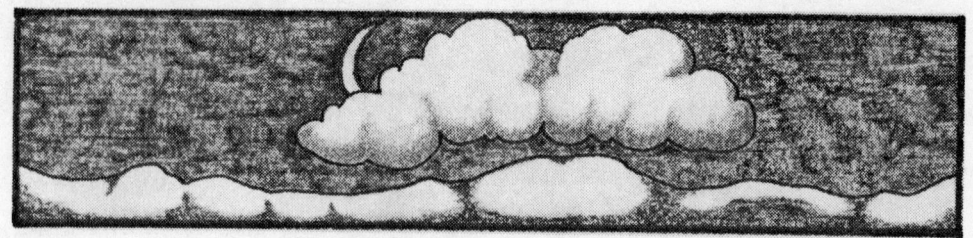

then spiritually. She was an activist, she was a dedicated seeker, free to invest her life totally in whatever she saw as worthwhile. She changes constantly, always growing, often confounding people who try to expect consistency or stability from her. As I look back, I can see that in many ways she is a visionary, for within her many changes and moods are periods of deep silence and introspection, and from this there emerges a clear vision of what to do. . . This gives her a real power in groups.

NOT LONG after I joined the Firehouse Company, Richard Scheckner and his Performance Group came to Minneapolis with their (dynamite!) production of *Dionysus '69*. Scheckner had a powerful influence on us all.

Richard Scheckner

We had arranged to do a private workshop together, as soon as they arrived in town. They came directly to the Firehouse. The two companies kept separate, unconsciously, one group sitting along one wall of the open theater space and the other group along the other. Scheckner came to the center, and marked off three areas with three large imaginary circles — doing a strangely intense little mime as he did it. Then he spoke — quietly, almost reverently, yet very forcefully and briefly. No extraneous words at all. He said, "This area is for physical challenge, physical combat. You must be clothed in this area. This (central) area is for physical exploration of each other's bodies. You may be clothed, or naked. And this area is for erotic exploration. You must be naked in this area. The exercise continues until any one area is empty. Then it is over."

a private workshop

It was an incredibly effective technique for bringing the two groups together. An hour later, the two groups were very close in so many ways: we had grappled with each other physically, testing each others' strength; we had explored each others' bodies objectively; and we had explored each others' bodies erotically (yet carefully, knowing still it was a stage, a play. . . It was exquisite theater, I felt. . .)

Scheckner's greatest strength was the intense, even sacred atmosphere of his rehearsals and performances. No visitors were allowed to rehearsals. Doors were closed. The atmosphere was very quiet and intense, conducive to a free and high and open kind of inward exploration and discovery. It's not easy to describe. His greatest strength was the space he could create: he was a far-out kind of priest.

a sacred atmosphere

I remember writing in my notebook at this time: 'We can create a sacred space.'

Even at that time, I had aspirations beyond the political, and beyond the conventional, but as yet the forms weren't discovered. But Scheckner helped: he came along at the right time, with his unique mixture of quiet sacredness and blatant outrageousness. . . He, as well as Syd and Marlow and Nancy and Carol, deeply influenced me. I began thinking a lot about the possibilities within the theater to create a deeply sacred experience — whatever that may mean for our secular culture.

Sacred roots

The ancient roots of theater certainly grew out of the sacred experience — that's what the Greeks were into, and the mystery plays and miracle plays of Medieval Europe. . . Is there a way, in America today, to discover some of the power and meaning of the religious experience? The seeds of my search were being planted. . .

The Firehouse: from psychological and social exploration. . . to a political force

Sometimes consciously, sometimes unconsciously, theater for the Firehouse people was a tool for exploration — at first on both psychological and social levels, expressing the absurdist awareness of the emptiness of material existence. . .

Then a shift in emphasis came: social criticism shifted into a direct political statement in our production of Brecht's *A Man's A Man*. Now we were using theater as a tool for open communication of political ideas, loudly and clearly criticizing the government's blunders in Vietnam, and the paranoid war mentality in general, and encouraging draft resistance and anti-war expression.

(I remember reading this graffitti on the wall of a john in some West Bank bar: 'War's all right — if you like bombing innocent women and children'. . .)

in the parks and on the streets

We moved away from the theater building out to the parks with *A Man's A Man*. From there, it was only a step away to move to the streets.

It was 1968, and a lot was happening on the streets — a new height in antiwar discontent and activity. And a whole new kind of life seemed to be beginning, and much of it was being lived on the streets, and on the highways, and in the country.

ONE OF THE FIRST EVENTS which generated an amazing amount of energy and which showed us some of the possibilities of political street theater was Syd Walter's induction refusal. . . Syd was a director of the Firehouse at that time. He was 33 years old, with a wife and three kids. And he was very gentle, quietspoken. . . He turned in his draft card as a token of his lack of cooperation with the government for their immoral actions in Southeast Asia. The draft board responded by ordering him to report for induction. Syd responded by deciding to refuse induction publicly.

Political street theater: Syd's induction refusal

Before the event, we brainstormed for things to do at the scene of the induction. We came up with the idea of a 'Miss Resist' contest — using the well-known old traditional form of a beauty contest.

We were on the steps of the Federal Building before dawn, a cold dark morning at a cold, dark building. . . Marlow appeared with a microphone — wearing a semi-see-thru plastic face mask with his hair slicked back, grossly greasy, in black tails, looking surprisingly like Bert Parks.

The 'Miss Resist' contest

Tony Maher was the first contestant. It was still dark. . . She slowly lit a wax halloween jack-o-lantern and raised it very high. . . it was all strangely intense, chilling. . . then, with great, violent concentration, she slowly tore it apart, piece by piece, totally destroying it. . .

Cheers, applause. . .

Then Marlow, bubbling enthusiasm, introduced the next contestant — it was Brigitte Hotchkiss, who was in a World War I jacket and helmet worn over a tacky 1950's-style formal (pink, yet). She recited a poem, which was a call for all the women to join the army — coquettish and cynical at the same time.

But the event became totally dominated by the next, and last, contestant. . . it was Carol Swardson. . . It was getting light by this time. There were maybe 150-200 people on the steps, protesting, hanging out, carrying signs, drinking coffee, talking. Several busloads of very young-looking farm boys being inducted arrived. They were handed anti-war literature as they got off the bus. Some authorities were getting uptight. And there were all kinds of people watching from the windows of the massive Federal Building — including police. Carol stepped up to this large, captive

Carol's naked gesture

audience. Like Tony, she had chosen to do a large, symbolic, wordless gesture. And it was incredible. She had an African mask on — wild and strange looking — and a simple, dark, loose-fitting dress. She stepped up in front of everyone and, in one fast move, dropped her dress to the ground. Totally naked, except for the mask, she raised a honeydew melon in the air with one hand, and a large, wicked-looking dagger in the other hand. She slashed the melon to pieces, violently, then quickly picked up her dress and disappeared into the crowd. The energy was wild — it had soared electrically when she dropped her dress. I could see police watching intently from the windows, and a few police in the crowd began asking questions, asking who she was. . . Carol was a person who would totally, seemingly fearlessly commit herself to whatever she thought was important. She risked arrest for this gesture, and that made it all the more powerful. . .

Carol won the Miss Resist Contest.

The intensity of the demonstration increased. We sang songs — one was a conglomeration of several hymns which somehow worked out together (sort of. . .). The energy was high. Syd finally came out of the Federal Building and gave a moving speech, telling what had happened in there as he had refused induction.

radical use of the media

antiwar victory

The event was covered by the papers and television. Syd and Carol were the heroes of the day. We began to discover some of the possibilities that Abbie Hoffman had been talking about: you can put any kind of statement on TV and in the papers, write it large for millions to see, if you simply present it in the kind of fashion that the media is looking for. . .

The event was in many ways a victory for antiwar causes. Carol was not arrested — no one who was asked would identify her. And the papers were sympathetic to Syd, seeing he was 33, and had 3 kids and all. . . The papers contacted his draft board which had ordered his induction, trying to find out why it happened, and who was behind it. Every member of the draft board claimed to know nothing of it — most of them said they were out of town at the time the induction order was given, and none of them would make any comment about it. The draft board came off very badly in the media.

Many people in the Firehouse wanted to plunge more fully into political activist theater. Others wanted to get back to more 'experimental' and perhaps less 'radical' theater. I was involved, with Carol, in the faction that saw theater as a powerful tool for political change. It was a time to make changes — many people could no longer tolerate the war, and American values in general which had created the war. We felt that the time for Saturday night theater had passed — the time was ripe for action, the government had to hear our protest, as loud and clear as possible.

A schism in the Firehouse: political vs. experimental

D URING THIS TIME, Tony Steblay invited Carol and me to my old high school to speak to the students about our views of theater. Tony Steblay was my former theater director in high school — a dynamic, sensitive and aware individual who had deeply influenced me. Carol and I felt that radical theater was something you *did*, rather than something you just talked about doing. Our views of theater were changing rapidly. We wanted to go to the people, and give them a voice — a stage on which to express themselves.

There were maybe 100 students in the theater of the high school when we arrived. First, we just got everybody loosened up, involved in the simplest, least verbal way possible: we put rock music (Jefferson Airplane, I think it was. . .) on the theater's sound system and had everybody on stage, moving, dancing. Inhibitions were thrown aside. . . We moved around and around in a large circle together, and it became very joyful, spontaneous. . .

Then the music quieted, and we said just a few words: we said theater is a tool for *change*, an expression of our feelings about something, an expression to the world of our ideas and ideals. We asked what in their situation as high school students was really bugging them — what would they like to change. The response was explosive: several people shouted, immediately, at the same time, "THE DRESS CODE!" It was 1968, and those young people — who were into the Beatles and the Rolling Stones — had to keep their hair so short that not a hair of it ever went over their ears, and they couldn't wear jeans, and the girls couldn't even wear pants of any type (dresses only, preferably with ny-

High School radical theater

a tool for change, an expression of feelings: abolish the dress code!

19

lons. . .). They had had the same exact rules concerning dress and physical appearance for several decades, and they were obviously obsolete. Many had resisted, fighting them in every way they could — and they had been suspended and gotten into trouble and were considered to have a 'bad attitude'. . .

Mass resistance (Gandhi lives!)

So we said, OK, what is necessary to do in order to change the dress code? We all started jamming together for ideas. And the idea of *mass resistance* was born — they could suspend a few, but they wouldn't suspend 200, or 500, without a lot of difficulty. . . The energy was incredibly high. . . Some people were excited, even euphoric; others were upset, frightened, freaked out. There were all kinds of confrontations. One good ol' football-playing type wanted to punch me out, calling me a long-hair freak. People were dancing, running, skipping wildly around the entire theater . . . and someone put that high energy music back on again. The energy exploded beyond the theater, into the whole school. We found out later that some kids ran thru the halls, shouting 'The Revolution's coming! The Revolution's here!'

High School Revolution

Then the students started grouping together, organizing meetings, shouting among themselves about demands and resistance and students' rights. Finally, the Principal arrived, obviously very upset. He stopped the music, and said that he had just received a report that several football players and other athletes were gathering in the boys' locker room, preparing to march to the theater and physically assault the hippies who were causing all the trouble! He talked with such agitation — as if mass violence was imminent — and said that our event was over. We were ordered to leave, immediately.

That was the first and only time in my life that I ever saw Tony Steblay really worried. He could easily have lost his job. He said we'd gone too far. We left, quietly.

A week or so later, we got a phone call from Tony that was a beautiful surprise: He was very warm and positive — and he *thanked us* for generating the energy we did, saying that, because of that afternoon's activities, the dress code had been abolished! It was a major breakthru for students' rights. . . And we saw many more possibilities on the horizon for radical theater. . .

I was learning a great deal, very quickly. And so were so many others. It was necessary in order to keep up with all the changes happening. I began to feel that my education had just begun.

My education begins

F ROM THE MOMENT I first saw Carol, I felt a crystalline, warm attraction to her. The first thing I noticed was that she was very, very beautiful . . . then I discovered that she was deeply intelligent — and sharp as a tack. . . She had one of the most progressive minds I had encountered.

with Carol

It slowly dawned on me as I came to know her more deeply that she was a visionary. . . A few years before she had been a housewife with two kids in the suburbs. . . One day, she heard Bob Dylan sing "The Times They Are A-Changing" on the radio — and she knew it was true. She left her husband, took her kids, and headed to the West Bank (Minneapolis' version of Telegraph Ave. in Berkeley) in search of a new life. Soon she was acting in the Firehouse Theater Company.

I felt very drawn to her — it was physical, and it was beautiful, and yet it felt much deeper than that too: it was as if an inner voice was telling me, quietly, persistently, "Hey! This lady has a lot to teach you. . ."

an inner voice

A few of those first nights with Carol still sparkle in my memory. . . I went to Carol's house for dinner. We started the evening with cauliflower and cheese sauce, Lebanese hashish, and white wine. By the end of the evening, Carol and I had become very close. . .

Then, one night after a rehearsal, some friends had a party. It was a quiet night, and not many people were there when we arrived. We danced together for several songs. At the end of a quiet song, she looked deeply into my eyes, looking at me in a way no one had ever looked at me before, looking in a way that saw me, deeply. . .

a deep look

She had beautiful eyes . . . which mirrored a beautiful soul.

21

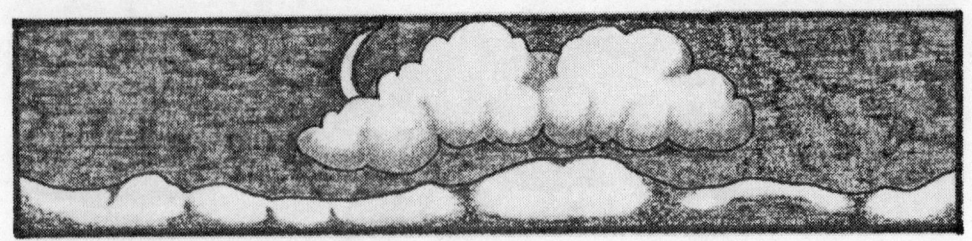

She asked, simply and honestly, "Do you want to sleep with me tonight?" And I said, "I'd love to."

We went over to her little house. Her bedroom was furnished very simply, and yet it had the quality of an exquisite fantasy — a few beautiful things, candles, incense, a canopy bed. . .

She looked at me, deeply, again. It felt as if she was seeing a part of me that no one had seen before.

a new lover

We made love — very gently at first, and then with growing passion. Carol lit up, fiery, strong, open, sensual. . .

Then we slept together, very close, as if we'd been sleeping together for years.

My dream had become a reality, and so very quickly. . . I soon moved in with her, and her two kids, and another actress in the company, named Muniera. Never before had a relationship seemed so meaningful. I didn't know it then, but I had found my first heavy political and social and spiritual teacher.

THOSE WERE THE DAYS of the Democratic Convention in Chicago, yippies and riots, Berkeley activism, endless, senseless war, marijuana and LSD, mass radicalization of youth. The Chicago 7 were doing some of the most vital theater around. So were the Beatles and the Stones. And the Living Theater. We were into the ideas of all of these people. I read Debray's *Revolution in the Revolution* at this time. It is a work of sheer genius (showing, for one thing, why the U.S. could not possibly win in Vietnam), and it had a deep effect. I read Cleaver's *Soul on Ice.* I saw H. Rap Brown at the University.

Change was in the air, swift change.

We had meetings in our house — some of which packed the house — planning for demonstrations, street activity. Carol emerged as a very strong leader.

I adapted a comic book story called 'Mr. Whiteman' (by R. Crumb in *Zap Comix*) into a short play. The subject was the white man's crumbling dominion of the world. We did it on the streets during the marches, with two blacks and two whites. It was powerful enough, shocking enough, for the streets. Gestures were huge, lines were shouted — techniques we had learned in *A Man's A Man*, and from the San Francisco Mime Troupe. In the end, Mr. Whiteman, who had been standing on the shoulders and backs of the blacks, is pulled down and falls, as everybody chants, "Yer just a nigger like everybody else." It had its effect. Some of it was even on the tube, during a newscast.

Then things started getting heavier than ever. . . During a rehearsal of 'Mr. Whiteman,' the two black dudes in it kept getting a little over-enthused — in my opinion — as they toppled white supremacy — symbolized by me. . . those brothers would get so into it that I started getting punched and kicked around. There was a wild, crazy energy — and it felt like things could just *flip out* at any moment, and I could be totally stomped to the ground. . .

1968: mass radicalization of youth

meetings

'Mr. Whiteman' on the streets

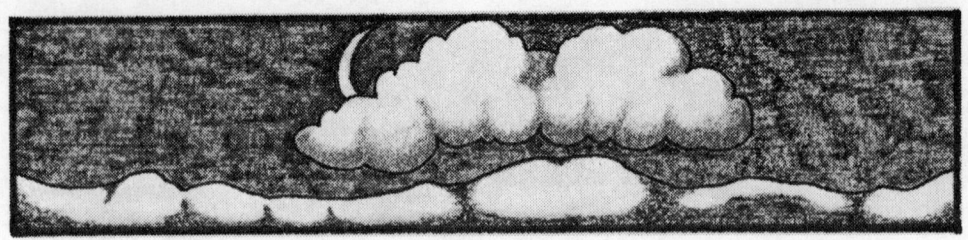

The play was getting confused with reality. . . And I was getting bruised. . .

Heavy days

THEN THE INEVITABLE HAPPENED: I received a very official-looking letter beginning with the friendly words:

> YOU ARE ORDERED TO APPEAR
> FOR INDUCTION

It came very quickly after I left school. . . I didn't know what I was going to do — all I knew was that I was not going in. . .

Induction blues

I went to a draft counseling service, run by young people committed to ending the war, assisting people in finding ways to get out of the draft, fighting a battle themselves in order to do what they felt was right.

They were very supportive and friendly, but they weren't too helpful. I was in too good physical health, so I couldn't get out on a medical deferment (like my friend Kent, who saw several sympathetic doctors and presented himself as having both back and knees that were hopelessly weak. . .), I wasn't about to go to Canada, and they said I wouldn't be accepted as a conscientious objector because I was not associated with an established, approved Church. . .

It was well-known that the Army was getting desperate, and drafting all kinds of people they would have formerly rejected. . .

For days, I worried, wondering what to do. The morning I was supposed to *report for induction* was rapidly approaching. All I knew in my heart was that I was not going in — I was not going to kill for peace — it was too absurd. . . I was not going to fight a war which wasn't a war. . . I was not going to be a military advisor for anybody. . .

I finally hit upon a plan. . . I was in 'radical theater' after all, so I figured that a piece of theater might do it. . . And I created one of the wildest roles of my life.

radical theater might do it. . .

I asked myself, what are the things which the draft board is most likely to reject? I found myself answering: drugs, homosexuality, and insanity. . . I didn't want to take any chances — I decided to create a role filled with all three: a

25

An insane Speed Queen vs. the U.S. Army

flipped out, gay drug addict. . . an insane Speed Queen!

It would make a very strange movie. . . Those were heavy days. . .

The night before my induction rolled around, all too soon. . . I dug up something I hadn't been into in awhile: it was kept in a hollowed-out copy of the Jessica Mitford book, *The American Way of Death*: it was a 'fit' — a syringe with needle points. (Shooting 'speed' — methedrine and dexedrine — was a nasty habit I'd gotten into in my last two years of college. I quit it — fortunately — as soon as I left school. But I resurrected it for this special occasion. . .) I had gotten a pretty large quantity of methedrine crystal. Between 10 p.m. and 3 a.m., I shot up almost an entire gram, and finished off by shooting several hits of plain water, just to mark both of my arms up — making all kinds of 'tracks', as we used to call it — ugly red lines of marks, made up of dozens of dots, each marking a different hit. . . My head was buzzing, tingling. . . It felt like I was getting a head massage from invisible magic fingers. . .

Shooting up

(Every word of this is, unfortunately, true. . . Well, who is to say? It may have been very fortunate, in a larger perspective. . .)

I had been told that they stripped everyone down to their shoes and undershorts (an odd, unflattering combination!). Somewhere I had scrounged up a pair of black bikini briefs, and some high topped, high healed black leather boots, which had a long, narrow toe and a Spanish heel and looked incredibly tacky. I put those on . . . and I put some really tight, dirty jeans over that, and a raggedy T-shirt, and an old French leather jacket. . . and I started parading in front of a full-length mirror, getting into my new character. . . God! I was almost starting to enjoy it! It was one of my finest performances. . .

& dressing up

All night — on and off, whenever I felt inspired — I worked to create my new character, the Speed Queen. . . I worked on voice inflection a lot — copying the half-feminine, half-Norwegian, highly contagious, quite outrageous voice patterns of John Donahue, a genius director in Minneapolis (the finest director of live plays I have ever seen, anywhere. . .). I worked on physical movements, getting very camp, very gay, a lot of off-the-hip stuff, walking and standing like a queen, like a lady. . .

A Queen is born

The evening flew by. Suddenly, it was dawn. . . I got on my little Honda motorcycle, and started it up. . . But I was so *fucked up* from all that speed that I headed off in exactly the opposite direction, right out of town on Hwy 7. . . Once I realized it, I just cracked up laughing, because I saw that that was my true, spontaneous, natural impulse — to head in exactly the opposite direction, right out of town, totally forgetting about draft boards and government orders and wars and methedrine and playing roles forever. . .

a natural impulse

But I turned around — I had to face it all, sooner or later, and I wanted to get it over with as soon as possible. . .

I got to the Federal Building, somewhat late. It was still chilly — it had only been light for an hour or so. And the building seemed chillier than anything else — gray, cold, austere, ominous. . . As I climbed the long flight of steps in front of the building, I found my whole body was shaking — I was really scared.

Federal Building revisited

But the moment I walked inside, I was totally in character. Look out, U.S. Army — here's more than you can handle. . .

Everyone was lining up, sheepishly filing into somewhere. . . It looked like the same group of straight, joking, young farmboys that I had seen get off the buses at Syd's induction refusal. . . I saw my friend Kent there — with all his doctors' letters in his hand. We were born only two days apart, so we were called to the same induction ceremonies. He took one look at me, and flipped. He couldn't believe his eyes. It was very reassuring to me. . . I knew I looked really decadent, really fucked up — too hot to handle. Fellini would have loved it. . .

I took one look at the line and headed off in the opposite direction, absent-mindedly, pretending to be totally spaced out — which wasn't at all difficult, in my condition. The whole scene is blurry in my memory, gray and unreal, surrealistic.

totally spaced

Someone stopped me, and asked me if I was there for induction. I started stammering furiously, incapable of answering, totally freaked out. . . They looked at me with a really sad and disgusted look and steered me back into the line. I had worked on a stammer all night. . . It took me at least 30 seconds to say what I normally say in three. . . I was

& stuttering too

27

a strange, dehumanizing movie

copying a flipped out girl I had once met on Nicollet Island, in Minneapolis.

We filed into a big, gray room, devoid of anything of interest or humor or human warmth. We were told by a fat, uptight, insecure sergeant to stand in a hallway, in single file, facing the wall, our toes to a line. He talked to us as if we were in the early years of grade school. We were told to take our shirts off and to drop our pants. . . It was a very strange, dehumanizing experience.

Soon everyone was standing there in jockey shorts and oxfords or tennis shoes — except for me, with my black bikini and tall, weird black boots. The farmboys couldn't believe that I was there at all. . . There was a lot of nervous giggling and frustrated sexual joking. It was a sad, intense experience for me. I knew they were going to a war they knew nothing about. Some of them were going to die. Some of them were going to be severely injured for the rest of their lives. All of them would never be the same. And all they could do was joke about it, to try to lighten things up, as if they were all back in their high school locker rooms. . .

Things were getting weird, and the next step was even weirder: we were told to pull down our underwear and pull apart our "cheeks" — as that uptight sergeant euphemistically called our asses. Then the sergeant walked down the line, looking up everybody's asshole, for some reason. I couldn't believe it! I refused to do it, and stood there, trying to be nonchalant (though my heart was pounding furiously), watching the whole strange event.

It was the saddest scene in the movie of my life. Putting needles in my arm was nothing compared to this: It was the first step in a massive and very carefully thought out series of brain washing techniques which would take innocent adolescent farmboys and turn them into killers of innocent people — including women and children — upon command of fat, insecure, over-compensating sergeants.

It made me sick. If this represented our country, I was ready to blow the whole fucking thing off the map — myself included. My stomach was reeling.

The sergeant came up to me. Instead of docilely leaning over, holding my ass up to him for his inspection, I was standing there, hands on my hips, looking at everybody

else's assholes, with deep interest and appreciation. He took one look at me and went beet red. Even his flabby jowls got fiery red. I could see the blood rise in his face, starting at the bottom of his double chins and rising to the top of his balding crew-cut. His eyes were glazed over. He looked like he wanted to *kill me*, and could barely restrain himself. He looked like a dumb animal. I laughed. It was all so weird I couldn't even be afraid anymore.

the sergeant

He looked me up and down, his fat jaw hanging open. I looked at him — he looked like a pig to me. . . in fact, he looked like some cartoon caricature of a pig, something out of "Fabulous Furry Freak Brothers" comix. . .

His eyes fell on my arms. He saw the red tracks. All the others were still standing, obediently, uncomfortably, bending over. . . He was outraged. He grabbed my arm and held it tightly and said, "Do you take *narcotics*?"

I paused, spaced out, and finally said, "Ye. . . Ye. . . Yeah." He shoved me out of the line, and said, with pure hatred slicing thru his raspy voice, "Get your clothes on and go see the psychiatrist."

Then he went on, peering up everybody else's assholes.

I felt a warm wave of relief — I knew the worst was over.

I went into an office marked Army Psychologist, or something like that — my memory isn't too clear. All I remember is a little gray box, with no roof, inside the big gray box. The man behind the desk looked worn, bored, fat, sad, pasty-faced, and half-dead — but he was three-quarters closer to being human than the last representative of the U.S. Armed Forces that I had encountered.

the Army Psychologist

I said, very slowly, spacing out and stammering and pretending to be pissed off at myself for stammering, "I wa. . . wa. . . wa. . . was ta. . . ta. . . told to ca. . . ca. . . come here."

I sat down. The Psychologist, or whatever he was labeled, said, "Where are you from?" and I said, imitating John Donahue in a very distorted way, "My *house*. . . You should see *my house*. . ."

I was weird enough for him. . . After a very short time he handed me a form, and told me to take it to a private psychologist or psychiatrist or something, and have them fill it out. . . And he had me take some kind of psychological

29

the sun and the green green grass

test, which seemed totally insane to me.

And that's all there was to it. . . I walked out into the sun, feeling fucked up and strung out and exhausted and free. . . I was flooded with relief. The sun felt so good on my face and body — I went to a grassy spot by a nearby lake, and fell asleep on the green green grass.

The Army hasn't wanted a thing to do with me since, thank God. . .

Those were heavy days. When would they end?

A crack in the shell

MEANWHILE, the Firehouse Theater Company was heading in yet another direction, whereabouts unknown, and I was still very much a part of it. We were doing two 'experimental' plays, *Faust* and *Rags*, which we were taking on tour, first around Minnesota, then to New York and finally to California, stopping at several colleges en route.

Rags was written by Nancy Walter — like most of her work, it is poetic, rich in imagery, deep, difficult, highly intuitive. At first it was quite confusing to most of us — it was not at all easy to understand what was happening. But as we got into it, its beauty and insight and relevant themes started emerging. It was about the youthful struggle for meaning, opposed by dark, unknown forces, which included *the father*. . . It was a deep and dark journey, an exploration of the subconscious mind, an initiation.

Faust was a journey as well. Its construction, content, and methods of production were wildly innovative. Marlow Hotchkiss put together the original working manuscript from dozens of different sources — it was amorphous, open. . . The basic structure of it grew out of Carlos Castaneda's phenomenal book, *The Teachings of Don Juan*, which we had all read. It was divided into four sections, in which Faust — a symbol of Western man in his search for knowledge — encounters the four enemies to the man of knowledge: first fear, then clarity, then power, then old age. Every actor played Faust at least once, and the ending was totally open, involving the audience — that is, those audience members who survived the rigors of the production — in a ritualistic washing of feet and physical exploration in a huge parachute which descended over the entire stage. Sometimes the endings were euphoric — incredible energy was released.

The journey of Faust in many ways became the journey of each of us, the journey of the Firehouse Theater, our search for meaning and understanding.

A journey with a theater company

Rags

Faust

31

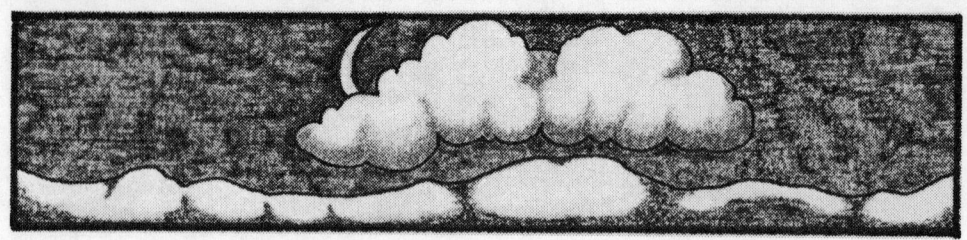

Yoga

Yoga means 'union'

A STRONG — yet quiet and subtle — influence for many of us started coming from yoga. The company had been looking for the best types of physical discipline. We had gone around to many different places, surveying different techniques, such as judo and gymnastics. We finally settled on a gymnastics class and the study of hatha yoga — physical exercises. Professor Arya, from the University of Minnesota — originally from India — taught us at first, and Syd Walter very quickly became amazingly adept at the physical exericses. So Professor Arya soon left the instruction of hatha yoga to Syd, and concentrated on teaching pranayama, or breathing exercises, and the theory or philosophy of yoga. Those of us who stayed with the study found some beautiful, unexpected results. The sessions not only became good, useful physical discipline, but had an emotional and mental effect, which started leaving us light and clear. Subtly, quietly, seeds were being planted which would bear fruit much later. . .

hatha yoga, pranayama

Prof. Arya

I found myself really looking forward to Prof. Arya's classes. I had never met anyone like him. He was a very powerful person — physically very strong, with a large, expansive chest — and there was a power coming from him which was far beyond the physical body. . . It was fascinating to me. He had traveled in very different worlds. . .

One day, he opened up the way to some of these worlds. . .

'Closing the Gates'

We did an exercise which he called "Closing the Gates." We sat with spines very straight, and breathed in and out very slowly, deeply, rhythmically for several minutes. . . Then we took a deep breath, held it, and blocked our ears, eyes, nose and mouth with our hands (with our thumbs, index fingers, middle fingers, and third and fourth fingers together, respectively). We tried to block out all incoming sounds, sights, smells. . . Then we let go of the fingers blocking our noses, so we could breathe, but we kept our eyes and ears closed, for quite awhile. . .

The effect was wondrous: I was plunged into a vast "inner space" — as vast as oceans. Suddenly, there were whole new worlds to explore. . . worlds I had dreamed of when I was a kid, but had forgotten. . . worlds of magic. . . worlds of the mind, created in an instant by the mind.

the effect of yoga: magic

I wanted to explore these worlds much deeper — it suddenly became more important than anything else I was doing.

I started viewing my life no longer as that of an actor — I was a researcher, and my life was my research project. . . I didn't know where it was heading, but I felt very open to it. . . And Carol had exactly the same feelings.

(Later on, as Carol looked back on these times, she said that her greatest strength was in her vision of what we *should* be doing, and my greatest strength was in plunging right into it, and *doing* it. . . We worked very smoothly with each other — we had a lot to teach each other. . .)

Often, when I left Prof. Arya's class, I felt very light — as if I was walking effortlessly and with a very different kind of physical energy. . .

Every day at the theater, we would do a long, free-form, everyone-to-themselves yoga warm-up before rehearsals. I could feel physical changes in my body. . . and, very slowly, almost imperceptibly at first, I began to feel changes in my mind. . . there was less tension. . . decisions became easier. . . I started taking life a little less seriously. . .

This was a subtle, yet severe crack in my shell of existentialism. Beyond were new worlds — beyond was a union with a higher force. For, as I slowly learned, 'yoga' and 'union' are the same word. . .

a crack in my shell

Seeds were being planted — and I couldn't yet even imagine the results. . .

F AUST was to have many unexpected karmic results, as well. As we took it on tour around the country, we had seemingly unwittingly developed another tool for social and political activism. There was a nude love scene, for one thing, with two couples. Minneapolis by this time was very much accustomed to the Firehouse's blatant

Going on tour

33

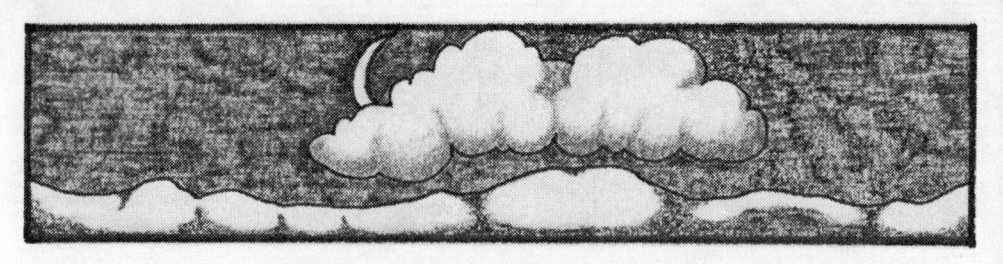

'indecent exposure' at Notre Dame

techniques. But parts of the rest of the country weren't. . . We toured to Notre Dame University, and were told that the Administration was cancelling the performance because they had heard that there was 'indecent exposure' in it. It is a Catholic University, after all. The students, however, were ready for change, for political confrontation, and once again we provided the catalyst. They organized the production in spite of the Administration's objections. We went on radio, talking about artistic freedom, and students' rights. Everyone should be free to decide their own moral standards, their own paths. Morality simply can't be dictated, not even by the Catholic Church.

The performance was electrically exciting: there was a lot of publicity, the large playing area — a gym — was packed, the energy was high, the media covered it and was very sympathetic and enthusiastic about the experience of the play. What really impressed the media was the intellectual depth and the quality of artistry behind our statement. It was a very different form than our street demonstrations and our high school events, but it had a similar effect — one which strengthened and radicalized the youth politically and socially. Freedom is always within reach, it's a matter of action at the right time.

There's a slogan of the AA that is deeply meaningful:

> God grant me the serenity to accept the things I cannot change, the courage to change the things I can, and the wisdom to know the difference.

That could be the activists' creed, as well as the alcoholics. . .

a revolution

A revolution was happening, and we knew it. . . and we were part of it, in our own unique way. . .

motivated by love

I remember reading at this time a phrase that has stuck with me, and has become more and more meaningful, even profound, over the years: Che Guevera said that the true revolutionary is motivated by deep feelings of love, for all people. . .

The tour was in many ways quite successful. We played for three weeks in New York City. . . The Big Apple wasn't nearly as dynamic and far-out as it had been in the past —

the theater we saw there was conventional, dull, antiquated, lifeless, similar to anything you can see on any night on TV. . . A few years before, that city had been a Mecca for theater. Now it seemed like a shabby museum. It was very depressing.

By this time I was very aware that the conventional theater of entertainment was not for me at all — we were trying to find new meaning for theater, to find old roots, to find radical theater: 'radical' literally means 'returning to the roots'. . .

Berkeley, California, was next on our tour, and we were in for some changes as we moved from the East to the West.

Berkeley proved far more radical than our most radical fantasies. They weren't *acting* the Revolution, they were *living* it.

When we arrived in Berkeley to do the last performances of *Faust*, the town was in an uproar: it was the scene of insurrection, revolt, centering around People's Park. A student had just been shot and killed by police in the action. Two others had been blinded by police shotgun blasts. We stayed right across the street from the Free Clinic, which was packed, treating people for bruises and injuries and tear gas inhalation. The day before we arrived — at least this is what people on the street kept saying — the police had fired tear gas thru the windows of the Free Clinic. People were outraged.

I was strolling down Shattuck Avenue one day — it's a straight commercial street (unlike Telegraph Ave) with a bank on nearly every corner. Suddenly, there was shouting and screaming and whiffs of strangely burning gas in the air, irritating the eyes. Then about 150 people, mostly young, but of all descriptions — straight and stoned, black and white and oriental and everything else — came tearing up a side-street and pouring out onto Shattuck's central business area. The energy was incredible. I was walking by two older ladies who were waiting for a bus on a street corner, standing in front of a pile of construction materials. Two very nice looking young men — short hair, neat dress, nice California fraternity-type boys — came running up to the women and stopped abruptly in front of them. One of them, very gently, with great politeness, said "Excuse me,

New York City

and Berkeley, California

People's Park

Shattuck Avenue

35

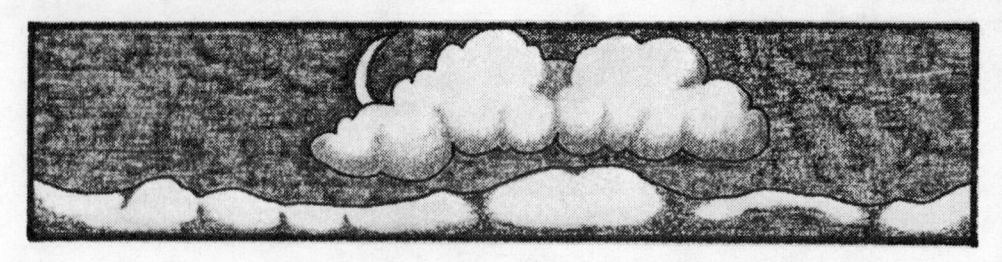

please," bowing to them somewhat while gesturing toward the construction materials. The women stepped aside, somewhat perplexed. The young man said, "Thank you, very much," and then he and his buddy grabbed some sawhorses and quickly threw them in the middle of the street, blocking traffic. Then they started grabbing bricks. The women stared as if they could not believe what was happening.

being trashed

Shattuck Ave was being trashed, as they called it on the streets: windows smashed, traffic blocked, fires burning in the waste baskets. . . Finally the police arrived, and the street fighters went running back up to Telegraph Ave to tear down the fence around People's Park, and once again regain control of it.

A few hours later, that street looked like some war-torn European city of many years ago. Smoke and tear gas filled the air. Glass and trash everywhere. Windows boarded up. Graffitti spray painted on nearly every available surface:

graffitti

Stop the war!
Victory to the Viet Cong!
People's Park
Impeach Nixon

The messages were written loud and clear. Of course, every minute of it had extensive media coverage. There was even an underground street paper called the *War Extra!* being handed out for free, which was full of information, tactics, and philosophy concerning 'the present insurrection'. . .

We saw that the entire city of Berkeley was consciously involved in a huge, rambling, sporatic, intense piece of political theater. . . complete with national media coverage. . .

we had much to learn

We realized we had much to learn before we even started performing in Berkeley. Much to learn about Revolutionary Theater. And after that, Post-Revolutionary Theater. . .

I HAD AN EXPERIENCE while performing *Faust* in Berkeley that was very strange, an experience I'll never forget — one that changed me, in a deep way: I *died*.

A strange experience while playing Faust

Every actor played Faust once or twice. Everyone related to Faust uniquely and personally, because Faust is Western man — and woman, of course — in search of knowledge; Faust is each of us. And the search for me bore strange, unexpected discoveries.

I played Faust first as a lover — naked, intense, not really finding any lasting solutions. Looking back, it seems like it was a very superficial view of love and relationship. I'd play it much differently today. . . but then. . .

as a lover

I later played Faust as he is hanged — the scene dealt with society's retribution, lashing out against the person of knowledge, and Faust's willingness to explore even death in an open way, a way that continues his search, even in death. I was dragged up to a high platform and three nooses were put on me: one around my neck, one around an arm, one around a leg. . . I gave a short, intense speech, and dove off the platform to hang, swinging in the air. I had practiced it dozens of times: all I had to do was keep my arm and leg forward and my neck back, and catch the impact of the fall on my arm and leg. . . But the first two times we performed in Berkeley, a very strange thing happened, and it was an identical experience each time: I must have caught the fall with my neck, because both times I suddenly found myself in another reality, though it was just as completely real as this one. I was soaring, flying very rapidly over beautiful green hills in bright sunlight. I looked around and realized I didn't have a body, and this was so exhilarating! I flew and flew, very fast, joyfully. . . but then I began to encounter air turbulence, just like in a rough plane ride. It got rougher and rougher, and darker and darker. . . Soon I was in a dark whirlpool, swirling downward, dizzy, nauseated, frightened. But yet I clearly remember thinking to myself, very rationally, almost calmly, 'Hmm, here I am in this black whirlpool, without a body — now what can I do?'

as he dies

suddenly in another reality

out-of-body flight

I started struggling violently, becoming very afraid, feeling sick. . . when suddenly there was a force beneath me, lifting me upward to the top of the whirlpool. . . I could see the top, from beneath it — it looked very much like the

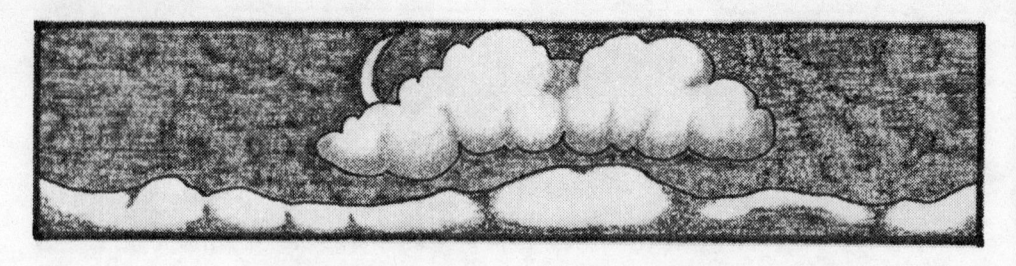

back into my body

surface of the water does to a skin diver coming up to it, with the light refracting thru, and dancing across the top of it. Then I hit the top, and came thru the surface, right back into my body. . . Slowly the reality of the theater came back to me — this thing which John Lilly calls our 'concensus reality' — and I realized that Marlow was holding me up in the air, letting me breathe again. . . I felt dizzy and spaced out, and it was difficult at first to remember where I was, who I was, and what I was supposed to do next. Fortunately, there was a long, slow scene that followed that didn't involve me, so I had time to gradually regain my memory of my life in this reality. . .

It happened two nights in a row. Then Marlow took over the part, saying that he was afraid that some day he might not catch me in time. . .

Tibetan Book of the Dead

Shortly after, I read the *Tibetan Book of the Dead*. . . It talked of flight in the 'bardo' just after death — at great speed, without a body. It seemed to chronicle my experience almost exactly, as far as I had been.

The rest of the performances of *Faust* had new meaning and depth for me — I was looking at everything in a strange, new light. The ending especially became very meaningful, where we sang and chanted (from T.S. Eliot):

> Teach us to care, and not to care
> Teach us to sit still

Death is a transition into a new and brighter life

I never looked at death in the same way, after that. . . Suddenly, I had seen and felt that death doesn't exist, except as a transition, a passageway to a new and brighter life. It is nothing to fear, at all — we are very much alive, even after our so-called 'death'. . . We are just shedding our skins, like snakes.

Faust was in some ways a genuine search, with genuine teachings contained within. . . But I began to find it somewhat disappointing: I felt that I was *acting* at searching rather than really searching; acting the role of the person of knowledge rather than really finding the techniques necessary in order to be one. Some inner voice told me to leave the Firehouse — whereabouts unknown. . . Carol felt the same way. We planned to go in the direction of political theater; we talked of getting a short semi-musical piece together to do on the streets.

But something very important was still missing, whether we investigated political possibilities or experimental. Our political efforts, whether in Minneapolis, New York City, or Berkeley, had often left me with the same deep feelings of dissatisfaction that the absurdists or existentialists had left me with. Both of those forms of theater seemed to me to be a lot like Freudian psychology: very good at pointing out the problems, the neuroses, but very weak at offering any viable solutions.

I started seeing the vision of the existentialists as a necessary stage to pass thru — one which reacts against and rejects the previous culture's materialism, violence, loss of ideals, loss of spiritual awareness, loss of magic. But where do we go from here? Yes, it's an absurd existence, filled with pain — but once this is realized, why continue the absurd pain?

We all knew that things were bad — a senseless war, police brutality, corrupt government, an absurd existence in general, etc, etc — so now what do we, as conscious individuals, do? Simply protesting, or simply waiting for Godot, is not enough at all. Neither is simply sitting back and being entertained, enjoying yourself, getting loaded, whatever your thing is that gets you high. There must be better choices. There must be a theater that is really meaningful, a theater which remembers where it came from, and so retains the vision and power of the religious experience, of yoga. . . a theater of light. . .

A new generation, with new philosophies, was being born — with a consciousness far beyond that of Beckett, Camus, Kerouac, and the rest. . .

Acting rather than doing

politics, absurdists, & Freud

a new generation was being born

39

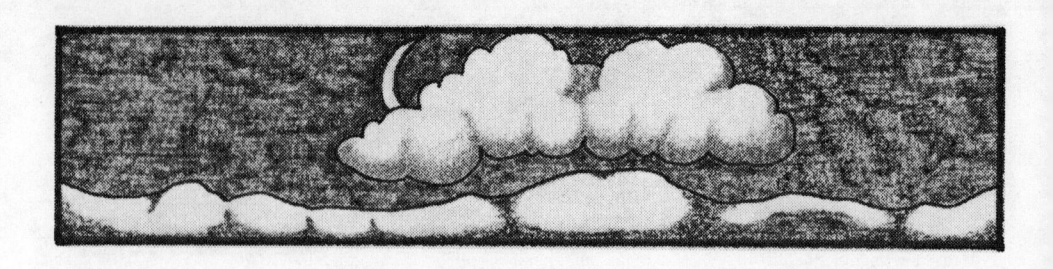

the path of yoga:

Carol and I found ourselves propelled more and more deeply into yoga, doing a good, long session of hatha yoga and meditation nearly every morning and often in the evening as well. And a strange and wonderful thing began to happen: the yoga became a quiet, yet powerful force, guiding our lives, answering questions, dissolving problems, pointing out a path.

There are an infinite number of paths to deeper awareness, to expanded consciousness. Everyone has their own, and it is constantly changing. . . To everything there is a season. . .

infinite possibilities!

Theater became a path with amazing possibilities — what is theater, anyway?

Yoga became a path with endless possibilities — what is yoga anyway?

Each is infinite. Each is whatever you create it to be.

a crack in the chrysalis

The crack in the chrysalis was now wide open, and a beautiful new light came shining in. . .

Part II
Days of Light

Theater of Light

The Floating Lotus Magic Opera Company

CAROL AND I discovered a theater of light in Berkeley, called The Floating Lotus Magic Opera Company.

I first heard of this group from Marlow Hotchkiss, who had seen them perform in Berkeley. He didn't like them at all. But his criticisms fascinated me. . . His main objection was that they didn't seem concerned with technique at all — the performance to Marlow seemed roughly like something a bunch of kids would put together in their backyard. And he was right, in a way.

a vision, light years ahead

Carol and I saw them soon after. I was amazed, deeply struck, deeply moved. . . We both were. This theater was visionary, years ahead of anything either of us had dreamed of. We both joined them, soon after.

Later on, as I got into Tibetan Buddhism, I discovered that the Lotus was doing a theater that was heavily influenced by Tibetan theater, as well as many other things, including deep meditative vision and fantasy. It was totally unique, as far as I know. I'll try to describe the performance in some detail, because it had such an impact — on us, and on so many others. It changed my life. . .

Bliss Apocalypse

The play was called *Bliss Apocalypse**. . . It is a long and brilliant poetic journey, written by Daniel Moore. Daniel was the guiding visionary light of the company: poet, playwright, director, musical director, dance director, master of improvisation. . .

He had written a book of poems called *Dawn Visions*, which City Lights published in 1964. . . He had been heavily influenced by William Blake and Whitman and Eastern, especially Tibetan, thought and disciplines. . . He and many other company members were *practicing* Buddhists. . .

---

* The entire text of *Bliss Apocalypse* was printed in the theater magazine TDR sometime in 1968 or '69.

The company which had developed around him was unlike any other 'theater company' I had ever seen, or imagined... I could not call any of them 'actors', because none of them considered themselves actors — instead, they were artists, seekers, religious pilgrims, musicians and dancers, poets and street people, yogis and freaks...

a totally new kind of theater

Marlow had been right in his observations: they weren't concerned with technique — they weren't concerned with most of the things that the Firehouse had been grappling with for years. They never talked of audience involvement, or of acting techniques — I don't even remember any talk ever of whether it was a *good* or a *bad* show. The cast was coming from a totally different space. Later, when I got to know many of them, and when I read *Black Elk Speaks*, and when I read Evans-Wentz's descriptions of Tibetan theater, I understood more clearly... But I was immediately and deeply impressed with the level on which they were involved in the experience. This was a totally new kind of theater.

The play was actual ritual, rather than acting at creating a ritual. So the participants weren't concerned with their acting at all — they were simply taking part in the ritual. And the audience of course felt this, and responded to it. It was more of a mass than a play. Many people in Berkeley came to almost every performance — they put it on regularly, once a week, in an old, decaying, beautiful outdoor theater in the North Berkeley hills called Hinkle Amphitheater. Many of the audience people would arrive early and meditate, often with cast members. Many meditated thruout the entire performance. On one very important level, the whole event grew out of a meditative experience, and in fact *was* a meditative experience.

actual ritual

The play, for the Lotus, was a *puja*: a ritual, a mass. It is a transmutation of the forces of darkness, the negative energy of destruction, into light, positive energy, bliss...

a meditative experience
a puja: a transmutation

The set was massive — backed by a line of large flats, wildly painted, with an all-seeing eye in the center. The playing area itself was bare, except for a low platform in the rear. Off to the side were the musicians and instruments: there were usually 8 to 12 musicians, surrounded, inun-

100 different instruments

dated by a battery of probably over 100 different instruments from all over the world, and a few from outer space: a huge gong rack, on which was suspended a variety of gongs, chimes, bells, etc; many different kinds of string instruments, including a sitar, sarod, zithers, guitars, a string bass; drums, tablas, congas, and home-made drums of all kinds; horns, including Tibetan temple horns — both the long horns (about 10 feet long) and the short, loud, reeded horns, called *galangs*, or *changs*; and all kinds of miscellaneous instruments, such as wood blocks, Balanese-sounding instruments, Indian folk instruments, weird pipes, etc. I don't even know the names of many of the instruments.

space music

The music was loose yet structured, flowing in and out of several very different styles of music: Indian, Balanese, Eastern funk, space music. . . mostly nameless, original explorations in sound. The musical effects alone were very effective. At one point, we'd build a very solid sound with solely the stringed instruments; it would grow in intensity, until it was an ocean of swelling sound; then suddenly, signalled by an actor's quick gesture in the play, it would instantly change to a penetrating, spacy reed sound — using only pipes and reeds. . . It had the effect of suddenly plunging you into inner space. . . The Tibetan-style music was very effective, too. I'll describe it later, when we get to the Family Dog.

I started playing in the chorus, and for fun I would jam with the musicians. Eventually, I joined the musicians for good. . .

opened with meditation

The event opened with music, incense, meditation — a long, slow preparation. Many of the actors arrived very early. Some got into elaborate makeup. Others did yoga. The incredible woman named Zilla, who played Kali (with intense energy — perfect for Kali) would get her face painted very early in the afternoon — a dark, wild face — and then she would disappear to meditate for hours before her wild, screaming entrance a third of the way into the play. There were shades of the Kathakali theater of Southern India here: elaborate makeup, actors meditating before and even thruout their performances. . .

It usually began at dusk, and was lit by torchlight — a dancing, beautiful visual spectacle.

lit by torches

Gradually, the chorus and the other actors would emerge, and sit in the bare stage, in meditation. Finally, they were all there, in a large circle. A chant slowly evolved, first in the music and then vocally. It was a Tibetan chant of purification, blessings, praying for the experience that was already beginning. . .

chanting

Everyone pulled out some corn meal from little pouches, and spread it in an arc around them: from the audience, raised above them, a beautiful golden mandala — a round, floral design — suddenly appeared around the people on stage. The mandala is exactly like the medicine wheel of the American Indians: it is a symbolic representation of the entire universe, and an understanding of the mandala is an understanding of the universe. It is a tool for knowledge.

a golden mandala suddenly appears

The whole play was a mandala, actors and audience were part of the mandala consecrated by an intense prayer, given in a torch-waving Prologue. . .

A central figure emerged from the chorus, praying for a vision. He is the Wanderer, and he symbolizes every one of us. The chant continues, building into the words,

the Wanderer, praying for the vision which unfolds

> O river of light, come thru, come thru,
> O river of light, come thru!"

and a river of light appears — symbolized, materialized, by a huge piece of shining silver silk, stretched out and waving, a beautiful effect — and from within this river of light appears the meditative vision, from which unfolds the entire experience of the play. The first personified universal force, or diety, to appear is Vairochana, at the center of the mandala, with his consort encircling his body. The Wanderer's vision has begun. Soon he must encounter Kali, the forces of destruction in this black (Piscean, *Kali* Yuga) age. . .

Kali is a symbol of this age

Kali enters screaming, running wildly, generating a huge amount of explosive energy. The chorus freaks out. The play loses its form. Chaos is rampant. Destruction is everywhere. This is the cataclysmic force of Kali.

The West, too, has long been aware of these forces:

> Things fall apart; the center cannot hold.
> (Yeats, "The Second Coming")
> The jaws of darkness do devour it up.
> (Shakespeare, "Midsummer Night's Dream")

a ritual death, a ritual birth

The play is a ritual death, and a ritual birth. A meditation upon the great forces of the cosmos: the forces of creation, of continuation, and of destruction — constantly interacting, a huge, ever-recurring cycle. . . The dance of Brahma, Vishnu, Shiva. . .

the Apocalypse, the great initiation

in which the forces of darkness are transmuted into light

The Bliss Apocalypse dawns as the forces of Kali, the dance of destruction, reaches its height. For in destruction is the seed of creation. Finally, the predictions are fulfilled. Five suns rise in the sky (symbolized — very clearly and effectively — by painted, fiery suns five feet across raised on poles 15 feet high). . . it is the Apocalypse. . . many images reminiscent of the *Book of Revelations*. . . Finally, the great initiation: the chorus forms a passageway, thru which the Wanderer and Kali pass, with difficulty. When they finally emerge, Kali is cleansed, purified, white, bare-breasted, beautiful, carrying green palm leaves, dancing gently. . . The transformation has taken place.

Now all are one, there is no distinction. The players flow into the audience, singing, chanting. . . many are playing zithers, with their pure, celestial sound. . . Audience and players are one, and they chant together, and meditate together. Sometimes the silent meditation that followed the musical, chanting part of the ritual would last 15 or 20 minutes. Then, bread and other types of food would be brought into the center, and then passed out for all to eat.

food for the spirit

It was not a pretentious, empty ritual of eating. Everyone enjoyed the good food, and felt the effect of the ceremony. People were very high and light afterwards. It had a definite, positive psychological effect.

a mystery play, a miracle play

Some people attended every week, and said that it was their church service. . . That, for me, was its finest result: it made those audience members who were open to it truly joyful, light. . . it was a meditation, on a very deep, meaningful level. It was a mystery play, a miracle play. It was a passage thru the dark night of the soul, into the light of a new dawn. . .

into the light of a new dawn. . .

It's impossible, actually, to describe Bliss Apocalypse. . . just as it is to describe meditation. . . It is beyond words, like a rainbow, like music. . .

Much of the journey that follows cannot be described in words. So don't take me too literally. These words are but a finger, pointing somewhere else. The Tibetans often caution: *Don't mistake the finger pointing to the moon for the moon itself. . .*

IT WAS NOT ONLY *Bliss Apocalypse* that was the Lotus's expression of a theater of light. . . It was their whole way of life, their level of consciousness. . . There were so many events and activities in their daily life which were beautiful, and meaningful. . .

The Lotus —

Like a full moon night feast in Tilden Park, deep in the woods, which began with several people running spontaneously around a large open field, then everyone joining the circle, singing, chanting, playing zithers — etheric strings. . .

a full moon night's feast

Or painting a huge mandala on the floor of their rehearsal space and living area, taking all night, and then going as a group to salute the rising sun with chanting, music, meditation, prayer. . .

a mandala

Or group morning yoga. . .
Or prayers before meals. . .
Or a trip to Big Sur. . . When we would find a place to camp, Daniel would first make an offering to the spirits of the place, and sing beautiful, spontaneous prayers to the spirits, greeting them, wishing them well, asking their permission to camp there. . .

Big Sur

Or beautiful Laura Allen, an Aquarian angel. . . She would play her zither like a celestial harp, and sing lyrical, spontaneous prayer-songs. . .

Laura Allen

All these things generated so much positive energy!

47

meeting the 'Star Children'

The night the Floating Lotus met the 'star children', I had a new kind of opening. Suddenly, the magic of every moment of our lives became clear to me. . .

The Lotus had performed *Bliss Apocalypse* at Esalen, in Big Sur — a beautiful experience, doing the torchlit play on an open field right by the ocean, with a full moon in the sky, preceded and followed by the hot natural baths coming out of the mountains. . .

Afterwards, we were invited to meet a group of people who lived back in the hills of Big Sur. . . These people were celebrating. They had just finished doing a ceremony with an old Hopi medicine man, who had given them the name 'Gayunics', which means 'star children', because the medicine man saw in them the fulfillment of their prophesy that, when the Hopi people are nearly crushed, white star children would return once more with their vision of a pure life, in harmony with the Great Spirit and with Mother Earth. . . They had just been initiated that afternoon. . .

We drove deep into the back country, climbing into the hills on ultra-funky roads. We finally came to a small settlement, on a big hill overlooking the ocean. They had a large fire going, and a big semi-circle with maybe 8 or 9 large conga drums, made out of old barrels. . . We set up our gong rack, and laid out many instruments. The full moon was powerfully present — the moon was in Aquarius, the sun in Leo. The music and dancing and talking and sharing continued til nearly dawn. . . Conversations were intense, and incredible. . . The moon set over the ocean. . . there was magic in the air, and everyone felt it.

spiritual street theater

We did street theater, too, with the Lotus — but it was very different from my previous street theater experience. We strolled down Telegraph Avenue, in Berkeley, with instruments — flutes and galings. . . one very strangely dressed person had a pole over his shoulders, and carried gongs hanging from the pole, which he could play as he walked. We moved onto the Berkeley campus, and collected maybe 150-200 people. Then we all sat down together in Sproul Plaza. Daniel sang a short, beautifully composed, totally extemporaneous, high, soaring prayer (his specialty! — like an ancient priest), and the entire group spent a fairly long time in silent meditation. . . then chanting OM. . .

Another time we set up our entire musical section in the Giant Eucalyptus grove on the campus. It was during some kind of student arts conference, or something, and a large crowd gathered. The music and its contagious spirit soon had everyone moving around, dancing, freely singing. . . Daniel was at his brilliant peak of inspired, improvisational visionary poetry. . . It was incredible. People were radiant.

The Lotus on campus

Another event of that time which was deeply moving to me was the so-called 'Holy Man Jam' in San Francisco. It was a series of events lasting several days, featuring many of the spiritual leaders from this country and from India. . . It took place at the Family Dog, a big space near the ocean, where rock groups often played. We were invited to do *Bliss Apocalypse* there one night. . .

and at the 'Holy Man Jam'

A very far-out musician named Malichi started the evening. . . He and his group had many Tibetan temple instruments, as well as specially constructed guitars which have sympathetic strings, like a sitar or sarod, which are never played but which resonate vibrationally with the other strings. . . They started the evening by playing their stringed instruments and chanting from the *Tibetan Book of the Dead* — space music. . .

Malichi,

chanting from Tibetan Book of the Dead

There were two stages at the Family Dog — one at each end of the large rectangular space. Malichi was set up at one end, the Lotus at the other. His chanting eventually evolved into Tibetan temple music, using long horns and drums. We answered his chant from the other end, also with long horns and drums. The effect was powerful — antiphonal music, like the Renaissance churches, like Bach. . .

antiphonal music

The long horns and drums are very loud, and the form of the Tibetan music is intense: it starts with loud, low, slow thunder claps of sound, mostly deep drums and cymbals at first, which slowly accelerate, adding more and more instruments, faster and faster, until finally they explode into total chaos. Then, within this chaos (unintentionally! — without technically trying to do it) a beautiful pattern of sound emerges, a melody soaring on top of it all, magically. . . It is a composite sound of everyone together! After soaring very high, the music stops abruptly, only to begin again, very slowly — this time, on the other side of the

a magic melody

49

good music!

space. It blew everybody's minds. Including us. It was good music.

We went back and forth, back and forth, seven times. And that led us right into *Bliss Apocalypse*. At the end, we did that long horn and drum music again, and Malichi answered. It then turned into a wondrous group experience, with both groups playing, Daniel chanting, everyone dancing and singing. The energy grew and grew, and finally burst right out of the building as everyone ran and danced down to the ocean. It was about midnight, and the freeform, high-energy celebration continued for hours. . . embracing the ocean, embracing one another, embracing life. . .

embracing the ocean, embracing one another

Many slept there. The rising sun found many people already on the beach, each doing their own type of yoga. . . each saluting the sun in their own way. . .

saluting the sun

I started becoming aware that we were all consciously creating a very different life for ourselves. There are infinite possibilities! — you are free to create for yourself the kind of life you want, if you but realize it. . .

you are free

Living with the Lotus: yoga, studying,

LIVING AND WORKING with the Floating Lotus Magic Opera Company. . . Doing yoga and meditation every morning. . . often spending the afternoons reading and studying — going back and forth between Shambhala Bookstore and the Mediterraneum Coffeehouse on Telegraph Ave. My capacity for study seemed to increase markedly when I left the University. I read much slower and more deeply, and retained much more. Now I finally had time to digest what I was reading and experiencing — something I didn't have time for at the University. And yet it's something so essential for any real growth. . . I read my way around Shambhala Bookstore, covering a wide variety of different areas — mostly Eastern psychology, philosophy, religious works. . . also books on and by American Indians, and the works of Jung and many of the Western metaphysical writers. . .

learning

During this time, I read *Black Elk Speaks* — it is a brilliant, inspiring book, in which Black Elk, a famous old Oglala Sioux medicine man, tells his life story. . .

When Black Elk was 9 years old, he was playing with two other boys near a river. Suddenly, he looked up and saw two men flying from the sky towards him, as if they were soaring to earth on arrows. They landed next to him, and said 'Come with us', and took him away into the skies. All his two young friends were aware of was that he collapsed and lost consciousness. He was unconscious to this world for three days. The two spirit men took him on a vast, cosmic visionary journey, which he vividly describes at great length in his book. . . He meets the six old men who are the powers of the universe, sees the vast herds of dancing horses and riders of each of the four directions, sees four maidens holding the four sacred symbols of the universe. . . And he sees many, many other visions during this time, which he later called the 'Great Vision'.

He came back into his body and regained 'consciousness'. He told his vision to no one, until he was 17 years old. Then he related it in full detail to the medicine man, who was amazed, and who knew that Black Elk was destined to be a great medicine man. Most young people have to fast and pray for a vision. . . He said the time was soon ready for Black Elk to give his vision to the tribe, and that everyone would benefit from it.

They made elaborate preparations for the ceremony, in order to enact the vision. The six oldest men of the tribe represented the powers of the universe; they painted horses and riders with the colors he had seen in his vision (white for north, green for south, gold for east, black for west) representing the four directions; and four maidens held the sacred symbols. They actually just chose a small piece of the vast vision to enact.

Then they prepared with sweat baths, and then performed it for the entire tribe.

While they were enacting it, Black Elk looked into the sky, and saw his original vision return, as it was being reflected by the enacted vision. So he knew that the performance was good. . .

The ceremony made the whole tribe very strong and happy. And Black Elk had gained power from the enact-

Black Elk Speaks

the 'great vision'

enacting the vision

gaining power

ment of his vision: he could now heal, and he could counsel others. He was a medicine man, a spiritual leader, and he became very famous and powerful.

we, too, have the potential for true ritual theater

The Floating Lotus was in some ways approaching this kind of theater. I began to see that our culture, too — like every other culture — has the potential for true ritual, spiritual theater, which unites and heals. . . That was what I was searching for, at that time. . . We may have to call it by names other than 'theater', like 'consciousness growth', or meditation, or group experiences, or group retreats, or whatever, but I'm discovering all kinds of activities which really affect people, in a deeply meaningful way. . .

Tibetan theater

I read Evans-Wentz's description of Tibetan theater at this time, too. The possibilities blew my mind. . .

The Tibetan lamas, or teachers, would do a pageant every year for all the people. It was a huge festival, with much beer drinking and celebration, and everyone came. It was actually a three-day *puja*, or ceremony of transformation. . .

a joyous pageant, a 3-day puja

A huge man of bread was baked, and placed in the center of the playing area. Then, in fierce masks and flamboyant costumes, the demons appear. They do a long, structured, symbolic dance. Then the deities and the heroes appear. The dance, music, and chanting continues for the whole three days, and in the course of it the magicians and deities subjugate the demons and force them to enter into the bread man. Then the bread man is overcome and destroyed with their powerful ritual daggers. On a deep level, *the negative energies of all the people are being summoned, called forth, fought with, overcome, and destroyed, transmuted*. . . The people understand this, and feel it. Often miracles occur at these festivals, including many healings. At the end, the bread man is cut into thousands of tiny pieces, which are given to all the people, and which are treasured, because they have the power to heal, because they have been blessed, consecrated by the puja. . .

the demons

are overcome by the deities

miracles, medicine

This is the type of theater that began to fascinate me. . . theater as meaningful, healing ritual. . . theater as it used to be, in some form, in possibly every ancient culture. . . theater which plunges into the depths of reality, which deeply understands, and which can bring that understanding to the people in some form that they can understand. . . theater which is a very powerful tool for consciousness growth, for cutting thru difficulties, obstacles. . .

Theater as *magic*. . .

I began to feel that my search had just begun, actually. And that my definitions of what that search was for were changing very rapidly. . .

Theater is magic. . . my search had just begun

I began to feel that in order to really do something meaningful in my life, I had to come from a place of deep understanding. In order to change anything, I had to change myself. In order to help anyone, in any way, I had to first work on my own head. . .

And so my pilgrimage began, outside of theater as I knew it. I had explored theater for answers, for truth — but I hadn't found anything. Not within our usual conception of 'theater' anyway. . . And so I gave up theater totally. Or at least I thought I did. Now, as I write this piece of theater, I can look at it all as theater. But I had to definitely, consciously, give up being an 'actor', in order to search for real meaning in this existence, and for magic, and for truth. . .

THE FLOATING LOTUS'S MAIN DWELLING and hangout was in one large room (with a mandala painted on the floor) which stuck out of the rear basement of an incredible, gargantuan, crumbling North Berkeley hills mansion. It had been a college at one time — Williams College. But now only two old men lived there, a man in his nineties, and his son, in his late sixties. They were into astral travel, and would describe what the other planets looked like, in detail, up very close. . .

The Lotus's Berkeley palace

Though the grounds were huge, and covered with forests, there were distant, affluent neighbors who objected to the sound of the longhorns and drums at unusual hours, and who objected to the lifestyle of the people of the Lotus in general. . . So we were evicted, with the help of a lawyer hired by a neighbor who dug up some old Berkeley statute which said that there could be only one family per house. . .

evicted (all things must pass)

53

Although they were on highly questionable legal grounds, we decided to simply leave rather than resist. . .

The Floating Lotus was a very good name for that group — they just kept floating thru the changes, always moving. . .

From the streets of San Francisco

There was some kind of festival going on in the streets of San Francisco. . . Many people from the Lotus went, with instruments, and played while walking down the sidewalks. At one point, where a crowd had gathered, one of them called out, 'Does anyone have a place where we can live?. . . especially in the country?'. . . A little later a man came up, in his forties, very spiffy, and said that he owned 1400 acres, primarily of redwood forest, in the mountains south of San Francisco, and that the Lotus could live there. . .

to the country

In a very short time, I was living in the country. . .

Here's a letter I wrote to my old high school theater director, Tony Steblay, after the Lotus moved to the land. It was written what seems like several lifetimes ago, by a very different person. . . Yet, for historical accuracy, and just for the fun of it, I'll include these letters, intact, and overcome my desire to edit them heavily. . .

a letter to my former director

Reverence to Madhava,
the Supreme Bliss!
Blessed by Him the dumb shall grow eloquent,
and the lame shall stride across a mountain.

11 Aug. 69
moon in cancer

Dear Tony,
I think about you quite a bit, and I feel a need to communicate with you — How's the revolution going in Hopkins? How's your head?

I've gone thru a lot of changes, and I *must* tell you about them. The chaos of the past two years (has it only been two years?) seems very ordered and natural as I look at it from this relatively peaceful distance: It's a cycle of changes: initial excitement, stimulation, creative energy flips over into disillusionment and stasis which in turn flips over into excitement and stimulation from some other source which in turn . . . etc.

I see this cycle operating on nearly every level of my existence:

my relationship with theater groups, my attitude towards different theater forms, art forms in general, drugs, literature, entertainment, the American way of life, politics, some people, my own lifestyle, spirituality, etc. (God, it seems like there's so much to say — I feel like I'm trying to cram everything that's happened in 5 years into one letter.)

I want to begin with the initial stimulation I received at the University (I could go back further, to high school, to the lifestyle you engendered in me, as it were, but you're aware of that, I think. Your existentialism, your theater, and your lifestyle have been a major and surprisingly persistent influence.) I remember four or five strong, exciting 'teachers' at the U., maybe more if I really think about it. But at some point — around the end of my 2nd or the beginning of my 3rd year — I stopped learning: I bogged down in academic life, in alcohol and — much worse — in methedrine. I wasn't learning any more. For a number of reasons. Some were personal: my roommate and soulmate John slowly drove himself insane, and I realized that our 'educations' weren't teaching us a thing about living our lives. Also, I had a bad bout with speed — methedrine. Never miss a chance to put down speed if you feel anyone you know is using it: it really fucks up your mind, it blasts holes in your memory. Speed freaks are vegetables: *speed kills*.

But a lot of my disillusionment with the U. came from the structure and methods of the 'great gray mediocrity' itself:

1) Students are *force-fed* material faster than they can assimilate it. In yoga they repeatedly stress that there are three stages to learning: (a) initial instruction and study, (b) a period of contemplation, experimentation and assimilation, and (c) demonstration of wisdom. At the U., we always jumped from lecture right into test — no time in between, no time to assimilate.

2) We kept reading about things instead of *doing* it. We used nothing except our intellects. (Mohammed said that the philosopher who hasn't realized his philosophy, so that his life is transformed, is like an ass carrying a load of books — an apt metaphor.)

3) In theater, we were taught an antiquated craft. The U. is at least 5, and maybe 50, years behind the creative forces in theater today.

This was really obvious when I started working at the Firehouse Theater.

The Firehouse, too, was very stimulating at first. Every word, every 'character', every technique of direction or performing was always questioned, examined. Very open communication. Wild experimentation. But I became dissatisfied there, too. Syd and Marlow don't want to focus on anything that is primarily political,

letter (continued)

a review: the University

bogged down

disillusionment

an apt metaphor

The Firehouse

55

letter (continued)

Rags & Faust began to depress me

The Floating Lotus Magic Opera Co. —

heralding the advent of the spiritual revolution

Star Hill

they aren't concerned with social comment, they don't feel that they know anything which their audience doesn't know. They want instead to keep looking into themselves, examining their psyches, going deep into themselves and revealing that to the audience. *Rags* and *Faust* began to depress me — they were so vague, so black and morose.

I kept telling them that I felt their images were too unclear. The workshops completely bogged down in a strange kind of psychic masturbation. We kept trying to mind-fuck one another, to trap each other in a highly intellectualized framework. Bad karma and bad theater. The amount of work got to me too — 6 days a week, all day, Spartan discipline. No time to live my life as a person.

While in Berkeley doing *Faust*, finishing my obligations with the Firehouse, I heard a 2nd hand description of the Floating Lotus Magic Opera Company. I wanted to join immediately — I think it's the best theater in the country. They perform long poetic ritual pieces out doors at night lit by torches. Sets and costumes are elaborate: much of the influence — spiritual, visual, and musical — is Tibetan. The pieces all grow out of the yogic experience, and their work heralds the advent of the spiritual revolution. It's a theater that freaks love and most theater people dislike: there is little emphasis on technique, the emphasis is on the ritual everyone takes part in. It's headed by a beautiful poet-director-guru-dancer-musician-painter named Daniel Moore. And the people in the company are very gentle and tuned in: they're all high, stoned on yoga.

Carol and I both joined. There's about 30 in the company — about 10 musicians, 15 actors, 5 technical people.

The play we're performing is called *Bliss Apocalypse* — the structure is the path of liberation; the play is an externalized, stylized expression of the meditative vision. Needless to say, it's completely unlike anything I've ever been in. Acting in the past has always been an expression of self: my concern is my character, my technique, my 3rd eye (which you made me aware of) focused on myself. But "performing" with the Lotus is in itself a meditative experience where focus is not on self, not on me-my, but on the meditative vision. . .

Now the Lotus is in the process of moving from Berkeley to Star Hill, an 1800-acre piece of land about an hour's drive south of San Francisco owned by an eccentric millionaire who loves our plays, especially the music. Most of the land is redwood forest — it looks like a combination of northern Minnesota woods and Mexican coast. Ten years ago, it was a sawmill. Two hundred years ago, it was a gathering place for Indians, a center for their rituals. Their chiefs are buried at the foot of the hill, it is said. Heavy, beautiful Indian vibes. And the stars are incredibly bright. I'm getting into astronomy and astrology as well as yoga.

Have you read *Three Pillars of Zen* by Philip Kapleau? It changed my life — and it's a good thing for young people to read, it's very clear and direct.

God bless you, Tony Steblay, you are one of the most beautiful people I have ever known.

I hope all is going well in your life. (If it isn't, consider taking up yoga.) All we have to realize is that, if we have beautiful minds, the whole world is beautiful. It's all in your mind. . . everyone is perfect. . . everyone has the nature of Buddha.

    Shanti,

          Mark

letter (concluded)

It's all in your mind

Tony Steblay gave me this letter, and two which follow later, shortly after I had finished this manuscript. I've changed much, of course, since they were written. But it feels right to include them, because they reflect those times in a much more immediate way than the rest of the book, which is looking back, remembering, writing from a very different perspective.

These letters really surprise me. Reading them now makes me feel as if I have changed even more than I had imagined. . .

AND SO, the Floating Lotus moved to the country. . . We continued to perform *Bliss Apocalypse*, for awhile. But the number of performances got fewer and fewer — it took three or four hours to get to Berkeley, nearly that much to get to San Francisco, and we had a great deal of scenery and costumes and instruments and people to keep hauling around. . . Finally, the performances stopped altogether.

No one was making any money, but somehow we feasted every night. I began to learn that when you're following what your heart tells you to do, you will always be taken care of. The Universe provides.

Daily life, rather than the play, had become the main focus, in many unexpected ways. . . Everyone lived scattered around a hill named Star Hill, on King's Mountain. It was a big, beautiful natural clearing, surrounded on three sides by redwood forests. We were told it was a place sacred to the Indians, and there was an Indian graveyard at the base of the hill. . . It *was* a sacred place. You could feel it.

Livin' in the country

the plays stop. . .

daily life

in a sacred place

57

the day's activities

Most people spent the mornings doing yoga, meditation. . . then gathered around the fire for breakfast, then worked on building their shelter, or winterizing some of the old dilapidated buildings, or planting the garden, or cooking, or whatever. . . communing with nature, learning the rhythms and secrets of its mountains and redwood forests and ocean sunsets. . .

the evening's fires

In the evenings, many would gather around a fire in a huge old metal teepee, which was used formerly to burn waste while logging the trees in the area. . . Each evening was different — group explorations, often involving music, or Daniel's ideas and words and inspiration, or Zilla's, or Surya Bhakti's, or others. . . sometimes chanting traditional Tibetan chants. . . sometimes just chanting OM. . . sometimes sitting in total silence — and on some nights, it was totally silent, all around.

and chants

and silence

a deep search

It was a deep search for magic, on one very important level. It was a search for reality, for truth. Many of the group had strong connections with many different teachers. Many were definitely teachers themselves, though nothing was ever said about it. Surya Bhakti (now known as Surya Singer) was a very light-hearted, and heavy spiritual force in the Lotus. Years later I realized the connection more deeply when I went into Daniel's room and saw that he had a picture of Surya on his altar. . .

books

I read many books. Many affected me very deeply. Kapleau's *Three Pillars of Zen*, and Krishnamurti, and D.T. Suzuki, and *The Life of Ramakrishna*, and Gandhi, and *Foundations of Tibetan Buddhism* by Lama Govinda, and William Blake, and Walt Whitman, and Carl Jung. . .

questions

I began to question quite deeply my motives, my *raison d'etre*, for my whole Theater trip in the first place. . . I remembered my first plays in the 7th grade, and the prestige and recognition they gave me. . . more people said hello in the halls. . . more contact with lovely girls. . . much more ego reinforcement. . . Yet, there was always some kind of magic, real magic, in the theater that I was looking for, even at 12 years old — and that seemed very worthwhile to explore. It was something bright and mystical and transcendental. But it was as if that real magic had been rapidly buried under confusing layers of illusion and cheap tricks and misguided values and superficial living and existentialism. . .

While living in the country with the Lotus, I gave up completely on theater as an occupation, as a path. I was no longer an actor. I became a seeker. . . searching for truth, searching for *real* magic, for real ritual — ritual with meaning, understanding, effectiveness.

a search for a new way of being

The first step was to let go of my past, in order to find a new way of being.

SOME STRANGE NATURAL phenomena accompanied the Lotus in the country. . . Natural and 'supernatural' too. . .

One night, I awoke because the earth under me was swinging, like a big rocking chair — and then I realized a fairly large earthquake was taking place. . . It was beautiful, awesome. . . My Zen studies proved useful — I felt no fear at all. In fact, it was exhilerating!

an earthquake

There is a wondrous teaching which comes in the form of an earthquake: nothing is solid, nothing is substantial, all things are impermanent and in constant change, even the earth under your feet.

(There is a Zen saying, 'Nothing is under my feet, nothing is above my head, and yet I am happy'.)

Then Bill, a very intense, wild, bull-like Taurus, came running up, saying, "Daniel and I have both had a vision — gather around the fire!" The wind was howling, but we dug a deep firepit on the highest point of Star Hill, and gathered around. . . Music, chanting, prayers — wondrously high and intense, blending in harmony with the intensity of the moving, howling earth. . . What a night!

And one day there was an eclipse of the sun. In the morning, after yoga, Surya Bhakti (whose name means 'Sun Devotion') marked off a large circle in the center of the open area with instruments of all kinds — drums, tambourines, cymbals, flutes. . . He started chanting, doing a puja of some kind. . . About 10 a.m. the light began to get very strange. Several of us joined Surya in the circle — the ceremony lasted about three hours, as long as the eclipse.

an eclipse

We had two mules then (one, incidentally, had been a movie star with Walt Disney in his youth) — they usually grazed restlessly. But during the eclipse, they both stood exactly at the same angle to the sun, with their heads turned toward the darkening sun, and remained completely motionless for hours, until the shadow passed. . .

sunset is a very special time. . .

Many, many nights we sat in total silence, watching the sun sink below the earth, into the ocean. . . The times of silence became filled with new meaning.

Zen meditation

Zen meditation became a source of powerful teachings for me. Within Zen can be found a key to the wisdom of the ancients in a form which is simple for Americans to grasp: you just *sit*, let your mind grow quiet, and the truth will emerge of itself, shining, beyond words. . .

we have the power to create any kind of life we want. . .

I felt deep change taking place — my core beliefs of the nature of reality were changing. . . I was beginning to realize that I had the power to create any kind of life I wanted. . . and there are infinite possibilities. . .

Light in the darkness

One night, when there was no moon at all, I was trying to get to my little tent... It was pitch dark, and I was blindly feeling my way along, when I somehow suddenly plunged over a 12-foot high bank that I had forgotten about and hit something very hard on the ground, head-first...

Light and pain exploded in my head simultaneously. Suddenly that very dark night was brilliantly lit with shooting stars and fireworks... I didn't know what had happened, and all I remember is thinking, quite calmly, without any fear, that I might die. I managed to sit up, in meditation, in a half-lotus, and I wondered if I was going to leave my body or not...

After a while, though, the light show dimmed, and the pain just became a regular throb, and I felt a large knob protruding from the side of my head... Nothing had broken, and I was alive and kicking.

I wasn't ready to leave my body, yet.

a dream group

Some of us started an informal group every morning after yoga and meditation where we would all tell each other our dreams, if we remembered them... It started getting very fascinating and very deep — with many glimpses into our group relationship and visions of the past, present, and future...

One morning, two of us had dreamed of policemen coming, and two had dreamed of ominous men in dark blue... Shortly after, sure enough, two cops came driving up — one with his arm out on a shotgun on the dash. They were investigating complaints. We had the feeling we were about to be evicted again...

evicted again

The Lotus splits up...

back to Berkeley

SURE ENOUGH, the Lotus was evicted from the land — our lifestyles were not acceptable to San Mateo County. There were many options open — and no commitments. The Lotus split up, and the people went in many different directions. Daniel Moore eventually went traveling to Europe and North Africa. Surya Bhakti went to the Lama Foundation in the mountains of Northern New Mexico. Some people (like Bill the Taurus) wanted to stay on the land, and live quietly, amongst the redwoods, leaving no trace... Several went to Chile, and took part in the Arica trainings, a series of disciplines gathered mostly from Eastern sources and led by a man named Oscar Ichazo.

Carol and I went back to Berkeley, drawn once again to its creative energy.

Ah, Berkeley... There were long periods, in those days, where I lived on almost nothing... At times my greatest source of income was the occasional quarters I would spot in the coin returns on newspaper vending machines...

I wanted to live like St. Francis, and have no concern at all for the material plane activity of making money. And I found it is very possible to live that way. Those years taught me a very wonderful thing: the Universe does provide for you...

> Consider the lilies of the field —
> They don't spin, they don't reap
> And yet not even Solomon in all his glory
> Was more beautifully arrayed than these

When I lived with communal groups, this kind of lifestyle worked perfectly... But I found, when I was on my own, that I started to feel like I was draining other people's resources. I was being parasitic...

At some point, I realized that, at least for me, some of my models of ideal lifestyles had been unrealistic. I had thought that St. Francis had simply left his home, left his father's business, and given up completely on material plane considerations. But it dawned on me one day that he had forged one of the biggest communal movements of his time, one that supported thousands of people. He definitely put his energy into material plane considerations, though from a different perspective than his father. . .

I still have a lot to learn from St. Francis . . . and from the lilies of the field. . .

material plane considerations

Carol and I were getting so close that people kept saying that we looked alike. Many people asked if we were sister and brother. . . It was strange, and beautiful — we both sensed that we had grown so much from being with each other, that we had grown to be like each other, to even look like each other.

I was deeply complimented when people would say we looked alike — because I felt she was one of the most beautiful beings I had ever met.

your lover is your mirror

After exploring different possibilities, and meditating at the Berkeley Zen Center for awhile, Carol and I left for Hawaii to study Zen Buddhism on Maui.

I didn't know why, exactly, but Carol had a strong impulse to go. So I followed her impulse. . . We got off the plane, and went wandering down an old funky dirt road. I felt a churning in my stomach — I didn't really know where I was going, or what was motivating me, or if I was doing the right thing. . . But the decisions had been made. There was nothing to do but to keep on walking down that road, one step at a time.

another step down the road

Zen

Maui —

a special spirit

Zen

CAROL AND I spent several weeks wandering, camping out, exploring the island... My doubts evaporated in the Hawaiian sunshine, and I was filled with a new sense of discovery. There is a very special spirit on Maui — it was the perfect choice for the next step of our pilgrimage.

We went to a small place in the ranch country called the Maui Zendo — a center with twelve students, who practice Zen meditation.

Zen is in many ways so simple, so intentionally devoid of outer trappings. Yet within the simplicity itself, a great depth and beauty emerges. There is very little instruction, very few words. Incense is lit, a gong sounds. Everyone sits, absolutely motionless for 45 minutes (difficult, even painful at first, but it becomes easy with practice)... then, another simple gong, and everyone slowly rises and circles the room, in a slow moving, almost slow-motion, single-file line, three times. Then you sit again. Another stick of incense is lit. Another 45 minutes of silence passes. Then there are three sharp clacks from wooden blocks, and everyone files into the dining room. There is a deep, strong chant, in Japanese. Then everyone eats in silence, gesturing if they want anything passed.

a slow, ritual dance

The life there is a slow, ritual dance...

The days are regular and structured — five days a week consist of regular meditation and eating periods alternating with periods of work — carpentry, gardening, cooking... One day a week is a full day of sitting and walking meditation; one day a week is entirely free. Each day has free time, after meals and after the work periods.

based on tradition and research

It was all fairly traditional — quite similar to *zendos* in Japan. Every activity, every element of the ritual, was the result of hundreds of years of tradition and research, calculated to have a strong psychological effect. Zen is a little like the Army — that's one reason why it works for Americans. Very slowly, the effects of this kind of life kept dawning on me... my mind would remain unusually calm and clear... people's eyes were often shining very bright, and bodies were strong and healthy... problems, difficulties would just fall away, dissolving of themselves with no intellectual effort... a tree in the wind, a flower blooming, would give an incredibly deep and meaningful explanation of the purpose of our lives...

the effects of just sitting...

a tree in the wind...

I saw what Hakuin Zenji — a great master — meant when he said that nature is really the finest teacher of Zen. The Zen center was out in the country, and we were glad of it.

One of the most beautiful things about living at that place was the presence of Mr. Katsuki Sekida, the Japanese man who was our teacher of Zen. He was a 77-year-old child, full of wonder.

Katsuki Sekida

He taught me a lot — much more than I knew at the time. He had a phenomenal, seemingly effortless energy, and a sharp, penetrating mind... He would get up early — 5:30 a.m. — and meditate and eat with everyone, then he would go to work in his little study and bedroom. He would spend about 12 hours a day, nearly everyday, in *concentrated* reading and writing... and he would do physical exercises for an hour every morning, and he would take about a half-an-hour walk every morning and every afternoon, and he would teach every night, delivering beautifully prepared lectures, and leading meditation. And his light would often be on way, way past midnight... And his door was always open to anyone who wanted to see him...

The main thing he was working on, at that time, was published when he was 83 years old: it's an excellent book called *Zen Training*.

and his Zen Training

Best of all was the way he took such a delight in all the little things — an oak leaf falling, an organic fig newton munchie, a simple conversation. He is a master — though he would never say so himself...

At first, the Zen meditation was physically very uncomfortable — my ankles and knees and back would tire... But Mr. Sekida said that within six months of regular sitting, your body grows used to the posture, and there is no more pain... And he was right... After a few months, I began to find it very comfortable and relaxing... The 45 minutes of quiet sitting began to go by very quickly...

Zen

I began to feel settled and calm in a new way. My body never felt stronger, and yet lighter at the same time. Mr. Sekida said that doing regular Zen meditation purifies not only your mind but your body as well. He knows what he is talking about. . .

There are two main schools of Zen Buddhism: 'Soto' and 'Rinzai'. The most successful Zen in America has been a combination of both. Soto is the simplest, barest form of Zen: you just *sit there*. There is very little instruction, very little guidance. You just sit there until you experience for yourself the miracle of Zen.

*Soto:
just sit*

*Rinzai:
the koans*

Rinzai involves the study of the *koans* — the short, often enigmatic Zen stories. The master gives the students *koans* to meditate upon, and they sit with them until they understand them on a deep level and can share their understanding with the master. . . Then they are given another *koan*. After working through an entire book of them, they are awarded the equivalent of a college degree in Zen. This is not as simple as it sounds — the degree is well deserved.

*a walk in the
fields:*

We often went rambling thru the country on our free time. . . One day, Carol and I were quietly walking across nearby fields. A horse came up, and followed us, simply and silently, close behind, as we walked. Then two more horses fell into line behind the first horse. Then a cow joined the line! Then another. Then some dogs! Shades of the Brennan town musicians. Soon we had a whole parade, wandering over the pastures, near the forests of eucalyptus and guava. . . We stayed together, always in single file. . . It felt totally mysterious and wonderful to me. Perhaps there was a very simple explanation to why the animals were following, in perfect order — but magical things were in the air.

*Brennan town
musicians*

*a mushroom
cloud*

One day, I was walking alone, thru the country. . . As I turned to head back to the Zen center, I saw a huge, brilliant, pink and orange and even gold atomic mushroom cloud in the air! It looked like the clouds from atomic tests I had seen pictures of — except for the shimmering, intense colors. I expected any second to feel a wave of intense heat. I thought that this life was all over, that it had finally happened: our 'civilization' had finally been stupid enough to blow us all off the planet. I felt strangely calm — no anxiety at all. Doing Zen certainly prepares you to die. I thought of Suzuki Roshi, the great teacher in San Francisco, when someone asked him what he thought of all the atomic weapons on earth and the possibility of mass annihilation: he said, with a laugh and a gleam in his eye, "What do you do when the atomic bomb drops? You become one with an atomic bomb."

a thought of Suzuki Roshi

But there was no shock wave. When I got back to the Zendo, there was great excitement in the air: the cloud was from a major volcano on the Big Island. The colors of the sky were so beautiful because of the volcanic ash in the air. . . and sunsets were incredibly intense, with wondrous color, for weeks after. . .

a volcano

WE RECEIVED A NOTICE that there was to be a large, all-inclusive, week-long 'Youth Congress' in Honolulu. Every group was asked to send delegates. I was chosen to go, with a young friend, 'Brother Thomas'. The week of the Congress was phenomenal. Boy Scouts and Girl Scouts were there, church groups and high schools, young Native Hawaiians and young white hippies, and Japanese, Chinese, Filipinos. . . We had all kinds of media coverage, from the beginning — this big youth event was taking place just before a national Governor's Conference which was also to be held in Honolulu, and it was understood that the purpose of the Youth Congress was to draw up resolutions to submit to the Governor's Conference.

The 'Youth Congress'

The participants were shy at first, until our first meeting. Then a beautiful togetherness began to blossom. Committees were formed. I set up a meditation room. The first night — and every night after, for the entire week — turned into a large, friendly, free party, filled with music, joy, even some occasional marijuana, beer. . . Everyone slept everywhere, often in large groups on the carpeted floor, ignoring the assigned rooms.

Many 'radicals' were quietly at work in the meetings. There were many speakers, and movies, and discussions, panels and group events . . . many speakers with many different points of view and interests. . . The effect on the

*another
'teach-in'*

group consciousness was amazing — it reminded me very much of the 'Vietnam teach-in' of my freshman year of college... Both sides of many political questions were presented, such as the seemingly endless war in Vietnam, the building of high-rise apartments and hotels on the islands, further 'development' of remote areas, and so on... But facing the audiences, the people supporting the war and the building and the government looked and acted like fools — they underestimated the maturity and awareness of their audience, and didn't communicate effectively with them at all. Some of them faced openly hostile audiences, and they couldn't handle it.

the last day

Finally, the last day of the convention came, when we all gathered together to make our resolutions. It was beautiful theater, very exciting... The Hawaiian youths began it, making the first resolution, with the young whites actively supporting. The first person to talk, a young Hawaiian, was an absolutely hilarious comic. He talked with a very slow, laid back style (someone said he talked that way because he had sniffed too much glue...), and had everyone roaring with laughter. A Japanese-Hawaiian girl gave a beautiful impromptu emotional speech, which culminated with the words, "We've been ripped off!"... The energy was incredibly high — even the Boy Scouts and the Girl Scouts were getting in on it...

the resolutions

The reporters were getting uptight. The papers and TV were shocked: they called it a mass radicalization of youth, a radical take-over (which it was)... The resolutions which the youth of Hawaii sent to the Governors' Conference included: taking the land out of the hands of the few big corporations and once more giving it back to the people, seceding from the USA and becoming an independent, sovereign nation once more, an immediate end to the war in Vietnam and Cambodia, making the 'Dillingham crane' the State bird (Dillingham is the biggest corporation in Hawaii — they're building all the high-rise hotels, and they use huge cranes with 'Dillingham' written on them, which dominate the Honolulu skyline...), establishing free-schools and day-care centers, and — this was the kicker that *really* upset the media — establishing a committee, which was a cross-section of all the youth of the state, which would work to put all these resolutions into effect, by any means, until the objectives of the Congress were completed. (!)

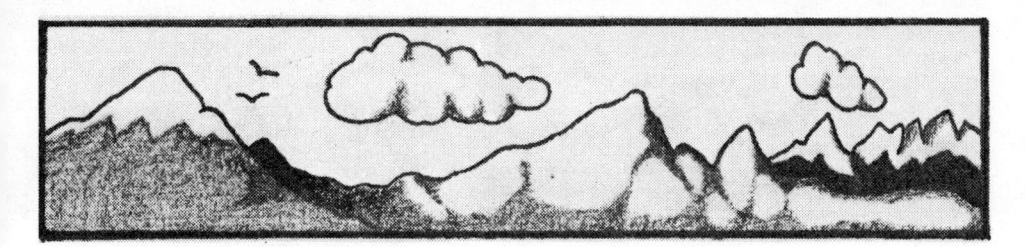

The more conservative kids were resisting some of the wording, etc., but the votes were always in favor of the resolutions. It just so happened that I found myself giving a speech which was the last one of the Congress. It was a plea, and a celebration. . . I talked of finding new ways of living, with each other, with the earth . . . of personal freedom, peace. . . There were many cheers . . . it ended on a euphoric note.

Let's find a new way of living, with each other, with the earth. . .

I still get occasional reports from Hawaii. The Youth Congress has not been forgotten. . .

HERE'S ANOTHER LETTER to Tony Steblay, which I wrote while at the Zen Center on Maui. . . Again, I'm tempted to edit it, but I'll leave it unchanged, for historical accuracy:

Another letter

                      Good Day Sunshine
Dear Tony,   11 Feb. 70
  Aloha!

More changes and comings and goings, of course. Hawaii is my home now, for awhile. Hawaiian sunshine — sometimes it's so intense, you can get on it and climb it, all the way to the source of existence.

What's happening in Minnesota?. . . Do you still have a job, and all that?

We stayed for a few weeks at an incredible free beach called Makena, on Maui. About 50-75 heads live there in glorious, natural sun, sand and ocean, often naked, long haired, very high, cosmic, funky splendor. They're all sea creatures, adventurers, and true primitives. It's the most on scene I've ever taken part in. Some people make daily fruit runs, others are primitive fishermen and divers. As we left, however, *Look* and *Life* magazines were there, interviewing and photographing and littering, so I suspect Makena may soon be a victim of media overkill — like Haight-Ashbury, Telegraph Ave, Greenwich Village, etc, etc, etc. . . On to new frontiers —

Makena Beach

Now we're at the Maui Zendo of the Diamond Sangha. We've been here two weeks, and it's beautiful, and I hope to stay awhile ("Drink deep, or taste not the Phrygian Spring," or whatever). It's a very disciplined trip — up at 5:30 a.m., 4 or 5 periods of *zazen* a day ("zazen" — sitting zen, meditation), a lot of

Maui Zendo

69

**2nd letter
(continued)**

work — we're finishing one house, tearing down another for materials, planting an organic garden, and collectively planning an arts and crafts center — possibly, hopefully, it will be a dome. We're way out in the country...

More later, I'm sure, but I didn't *really* write to rap about this zendo — I really wrote to announce to you and to the world in general that —

**The Revolution
has been won**

The Revolution has been won!
(Right on!)
(Getting it on!)
(Getting it together!)

You probably know it, actually, most everyone does — but it's good to make a formal announcement of the fact.

The Revolution has been won because the Revolution is all in our minds, and once we grasp this fact, the Revolution has been won.

Now, all we have to do is to live fully the post-Revolutionary life. No more Revolutionary rhetorical violent bullshit, no more fighting and pig-hating and martyrdom — just get it on! "In order to live in a beautiful world," says Swami Satchidananda, "simply make your head a beautiful place." Make a joyful noise unto the Lord.

'In order to live in a beautiful world, make your head a beautiful place.'

I've traveled a lot recently — Minneapolis to San Francisco, back to Mpls, east on tour with the Firehouse, first around Minnesota — St. John's and St. Benedict's and even Hamline — then to Notre Dame and Philadelphia, and New York City, and then to some far-out, flipped out Eastern colleges — Bennington and Smith — then back to Minnesota, via the Madison Revolution, then a smashing stone-soul drive to California via Idaho and Washington, on to the Berkeley violent revolution, on to Big Sur and Star Hill with the Floating Lotus Magic Opera Company, then to San Francisco, staying at the Firehouse mansion, back to Minneapolis, back to Frisco, and now to Hawaii.

And *everywhere*, people are getting into the post-Revolutionary life, gettin it on — complete non-violence, total acceptance of people (which means total acceptance of yourself, first of all), healthy, positive minds, and, yes, *love*. And Mother Earth. Cosmic consciousness. Liberation is here and now.

Pardon my euphoria. Carol and I just climbed a big, sharp hill — must be volcanic — stompin thru the jungle, making love on the top, with an intense sun and heavy, almost stormy wind off the ocean, and a shimmery, radiant view of the whole north side of Maui, from the ocean on two sides to the Haleakala crater, reflecting the ocean in a misty, radiant sheath of light, 12,000 feet above. Incredible. Hawaii is a vision.

But I'm wandering a bit. All I really wanted to do is to rap about a few of the things which have convinced me that the Revolution has been won, a few of the many guides I've encountered on my trip, in a random order, as they come to me. . .

All kinds of different ways, shapes, sizes, forms, happenings. . .

Floating Lotus Magic Opera Company — One of the highest theatrical experiences imaginable. It begins and ends with chanting and meditation. The entire play is, on one level, a vision of Awakening in meditation: first the river of light appears, then the powers of Vairocana appear, eventually the goddess Kali appears — the forces of change, destruction, death — and she is finally transformed into the life-giving powers of illumination.

It's *incredible*. Much of the play is based on the Tibetan mystery plays: the basic theme — overcoming the powers of darkness, spiritual transformation — the characters — archtypal, huge masks, stylized movement — the stoned visual effects — fire engulfing the universe, mountains rising out of the sea, five suns rising — and the stoned Tibetan music — longhorns, huge drums, gongs. The music also had Balanese, Indian, and a hundred other influences. . .

It was such a high, real, meaningful experience for actors, audience, and musicians. . . everyone. . .

And just as often the Lotus simply did totally open, unstructured events, celebrations, ecstatic group rituals, such as *"Ritual Celebration of our Breath on the Mandala of this Earth."* The Lotus-force, with its deep roots in Tibetan Buddhism, gets more people together on higher levels than I've ever thought possible, thru meditation, cosmic music, free dance, words — sometimes — of archtypal splendor (Daniel Moore is one of the best poets I know of). . . words like,

"swift interstellar sperm swimmer, expanding, unfolding, green serpent of the Universes"

and —

"Father! Mother!
In the center of space
Fucking your light into existence —
Their orgasms
vibrate
now
in the center of your molecules!"

Words you can touch and feel.

2nd letter to Tony:
I've encountered many guides on this trip:

The Lotus:

mad ecstatics

words from Bliss Apocalypse

71

2nd letter to Tony (continued)

A tantric space trip. We never rehearsed, we never performed. We'd just gather, meditate in silence, chant "Om Mani Padme Hum!" — "Hail to the Jewel of Bliss in the Lotus of Consciousness" — and the high from the meditation and chanting would carry into music and physical expression and sometimes poetry and it would all just start to flow, a moving swirling mandala, a metaphor of existence.

The Living Theater is revolutionary. The Lotus is post-revolutionary.

Zen meditation

Zazen — Zazen (Zen meditation), like a sunrise or sunset, is a fragile thing to talk about. All I want to say is that its effects are immediate. And I want to share a few jewels from the *Shodoka* and from Dogen Zengi. *Shodoka* — 8th c. Chinese zen (rather, "c'han") poem:

Zen teachings

No bad fortune, no good fortune, no loss, no gain;
Never seek such things in the Nirvana mind.
For years the dusty mirror has gone uncleaned.
Now let us polish it completely, once and for all. . .

Release your hold on earth, water, fire, wind;
Drink and eat as you wish in the Nirvana mind;
All things are transient and completely empty—
This is the great enlightenment of Shakyamuni Buddha. . .

Walking and sitting — both of these are Zen;
Speaking or silent, active or quiet, our body is at peace.
Even facing the sword of death, our mind is unmoved;
Even drinking poison, our mind is quiet. . .

Right here it is eternally full and complete;
If you search elsewhere, you cannot see it.
You cannot grasp it, you cannot reject it;
In the midst of not gaining, in that condition you gain it."

Dogen Zengi is "almost our only teacher," according to Robert Aitkin, one of the leaders here, who's been into Zen for 20-some years. Dogen lived in Kamakura, Japan. Sit with these words awhile:

key words

"To study Buddhism is to study the self.
To study the self is to forget the self.
To forget the self is to become identified with all things.
To be identified with all things is to be Truth itself,
   free from attachment
      to oneself and to others."

Buddhist world view — Everything is subjective — there is no "objective reality" as we normally conceive of it. It's all in our minds — that's why the Revolution has been won. In zazen, "pure subjectivity becomes pure objectivity." This belief has really, literally, turned my head around.

2nd letter (continued) Buddhist world view

Mr. Sekida's writings — Katsuki Sekida is our spiritual leader here at the Maui Zendo — he's a radiant and serene 76 year old Japanese monk (I later found out that he is a married layman) currently at work translating his writings into English. His writing is excellent — very specific and very *physical*, always directed toward achieving what he calls "absolute samadhi."

Carol once said "I used to read for a lot of different reasons — pleasure, some kind of knowledge, facts — now I read to change my life." Right on.

Here are some of Mr. Sekida's words which I sent to Kent upon receiving a most eloquent, even poetic, letter plunged into Samuel Beckett — TS Eliot — "mad clinitian of human experience" — black — even beat generation *despair*. He's on a bummer again. "Thrownness."

From "Pure Existence": (a post-revolutionary article) by Katsuki Sekida:

"*Thrownness* is the term that appears in Martin Heidegger's *Being and Time*. No one seems to take it as a disease and an object of possible remedy, and Heidegger seems to accept it as the basic mood of Dasein (the name of the character Heidegger examines). . .

"Many present-day intellectuals feel they are given their seats in this troubled world against their wills. In that respect, 'thrownness' can certainly be called their basic mood. . .

"Those who are suffering from mental troubles often do not realize they are suffering from illness as others may when subjected to physical disorders. Indeed, almost all people are suffering from nervous disorders, and almost all people think of the mind as naturally that way, and never think of a remedy. Literature is the mirror of the human mind. All sufferings which appear in the world of literature are of mental disorder, yet the characters in modern novels do not seem to think so. . . Nevertheless, it is a fever of the mind. People die of mental illness as they die of physical diseases. Physical disease is attended by a monitor called the mind. In mental illness, the monitor himself is subjected to the disease. He is deranged, and helplessly leads his own destiny to ultimate destruction.

Mr. Sekida's writings

'Pure Existence': the Eastern mind examines the Western mind

'almost all people are suffering from nervous disorders'

true freedom

"True freedom of mind consists in not being dragged on by one's own mind. To be free from one's own mind makes true freedom of the mind — genuine free will. The environment is mere accompaniment."

I feel very grateful that I'm able to come into contact with a mind and soul like Mr. Sekida's — his writings have affected me nearly as much as his talks, which have affected me nearly as much as his presence. . .

ever-accelerating development of human consciousness

Last night, he talked about the ever-accelerating development of human consciousness, saying that now in one year, the development of our consciousness is equal to perhaps 1000 years of development in past times. Then he tripped out with the wonderful potential we now have, if we only grasp it, if we only realize it.

I can't describe in words, really, the effect of his presence. So serene and peaceful and detached, and at the same time, so incredibly focused, tuned in. He shows us how Zen can lead to self-mastery.

"The miracle of Zen is peace of mind," he says.

the Guyunics at Big Sur

An Aquarius Moon night — When the full moon was in Aquarius, five full moons ago, I was with the Floating Lotus and we had a rendevous with the Guyunics, the "Sky Children," who live in the hills of Big Sur. They're mostly young earth people scattered all over the hills, some own land and some don't, and they had just gone thru a ceremony with a Hopi medicine man, who saw in these people the reincarnation of his people. The Indian Earth Spirit arising.

There was constant music thruout the night. Nearly everyone played at some time or other — there was a large half-circle of 7 or 8 big conga drums and a large gong rack (like Christopher Tree — ever heard him play his gongs?) and all kinds of other instruments. We were on the top of a hill, overlooking the ocean. The music made it all happen so much more intensely. The music made it all happen —

I talked with Amelia. She was the mother of them all. Other people — townspeople — had said she was a witch. I've discovered that being a witch is a good thing: *witch* and *wise* come from the same root word. . . We talked about getting land, and having children. That's the level they're living on — that's a post-revolutionary life. Amelia is very beautiful, long flaming wild silvery white hair. We were by a large fire, and it was the first time I ever felt a rising sexual attraction for someone who must be 50 years old. She spoke very softly, yet with so much love and strength and vibrant positive energy —

Later I talked with someone named Elf Friend. By now we were indoors in a beautiful warm funky house with a whole wall filled with hanging musical instruments, including a sitar. There was an incredibly lovely, very young blonde Aquarius girl playing a zither and singing music that charged the atmosphere with something very bright and magical. Her name is Laura Allen, and she is an Aquarian angel.

2nd letter to Tony (continued)

Amelia: silvery white witch

Elf Friend

Laura Allen

The wonder of it all, the wonder of the future, which is the wonder of a vision of what this present moment really is, arose within me. The joy of following the path that has heart. It was so exhilerating. So many fantastical things came down that night.

I kept thinking of Tom Olson thruout that night. Do you know him? He is a wild movie maker and writer I lived with for awhile in a large communal house — the 'Eater House' — in St. Paul.

After the dawn had become silent, and the rooster cries had risen into the sky (with rose colored fingers), I began to write to him. I thought mostly of one night in St. Paul when Tom had a vision of the future/present and was euphoric, ecstatic all night. He saw it all beginning to happen. I saw Tom just briefly that night, and he was radiant, telling about the Apocalypse, about huge sweeping change, that's happening now.

Tom's spirit buoyed up my spirit all that night. His vision of beauty and creative anarchy is being realized. At Big Sur, and northern California, and Georgeville Minnesota, and Maui, and everywhere. It's all in our minds.

To live in a beautiful world, we just have to get our heads in a beautiful place.

the wonder of this moment

Tom Olson, movie-maker, writer, visionary

2nd letter to Tony (continued)

Maybe I should end this letter here, because in a sense, I'm just saying the same thing over and over. But in another sense, there's so much to say... So I'll keep on truckin — after some meditation and some music...

So much to say... But I'm running out of words. I'll just briefly mention a few of the other things lately that have blown my mind...

Bucky Fuller

Buckminster Fuller — says he realized in 1928 that it was no longer necessary to work for a living — in our modern mechanized society, all those values (which our parents still cling to) are out-dated. So he carefully looked around, and tried to discover what *needed* to be done, what we were neglecting. An ultra-post-revolutionary attitude. So he got into environment and ecology and *An Operation Manual for Space Ship Earth* and design, geodesic domes, etc. And he was silent for two or three years. And when he started talking and writing, he sounded like no one else, before or since...

Music

Music! — What is there to say? The Music is the Message.

Karma

The Law of Karma — For every good vibration you put out, you get a good vibe back. For every bad vibe you put out, you get a bad vibe back. The way of the world.

I'm into a Zen trip, a disciplined trip... I'm into carpentry, and a lot of things I've never been into. And I've deserted theater, maybe permanently. If I ever get back into performing again, I may be doing just music. Actually, I'm still in theater — the theater of life.

But it's impossible for me to project into the future these days. I don't know, I may be here quite awhile...

2nd letter (concluded)

Carol and I are still together, but in a new way — we're trying not to put any possessive ego trips on each other. We're letting each other have much more space. And we're both trying to find the strength to be alone much more. She's leaving for California soon — probably about two weeks — in order to buy land. Most of it is already arranged. There's a beautiful scene developing now in northern California, where we've found land possibilities. There's a lot of pioneers up there, living in domes and teepees.

I'm gonna send this off to you before I think about it too much longer. . .

Peace, my friend. . .

>Keep the faith,
>Keep in touch
>
>   Love,
>   Mark

prophets

AFTER SEVERAL MONTHS at the Zen Center, hearing no music from an electronic source, someone brought a portable tape recorder and a tape of the Beatles' latest record, 'Abbey Road'. Listening to it was an experience of deep joy. . . They are prophets. . . All you need is love.

Carol and I

Carol and I had been in some ways growing apart, and in some ways just getting into ourselves, while at the Zen Center. . . The atmosphere didn't seem at all conducive to relationships — everything was geared to inner work, to meditation. We had grown so much from being together. But now, things had changed — we both felt that our growth was now taking place within each of us, in the silence of our own being. We were no longer learning primarily from each other — we were learning from ourselves.

splitting up

After a few months, Carol said she wanted to go back to the Mainland, and get a group together, and get land in the country. I felt torn — I wanted to stay on Maui, and yet I wanted to go with her. I loved her energy, I loved being around her. Yet, I felt in my heart that I should stay — I was growing, deepening in new ways . . . and I had just begun to really get into Zen.

Carol left, very quickly. I watched her go walking down the dusty road, with a little pack thrown over her shoulder, no more. . . I felt an impulse to run after her, to go with her, or to beg her to stay. Yet an inner voice said to just let her go. . . I watched her walk down the road — and she didn't look back. A voice in my head sang the words from an old blues song,

> Let her go, let her go,
> God bless her. . .
> Wherever she may be. . .

A gong rang, and it was time for meditation. I went in and sat down, in silence. I became aware that I was in a state of intense agitation — and I hadn't even realized it before. I was furiously throwing contradicting questions and commands at myself — 'What are you doing?' 'Why are you staying?' 'Let her go!' 'Go get her!' 'Why are you letting her slip away?' 'Don't you love her?' etc, etc, at a mile a minute. . .

contradicting questions

Then, a surprising thing happened. . . As I sat there, motionless, just watching all this activity in my head, I felt a sudden, huge wave of relief, almost as if a storm had broken over me, and all the questions and tension suddenly dissolved. . . It was in some strange way like a huge egg which broke over my head, and bathed my whole body in something calming and relaxing and freeing. . . Suddenly, in a moment, there was no problem at all: Carol needed the space to do what she must do, and I needed the space to do what I must do. It was perfect. And I felt very connected with her, even though we had just separated. I saw that I didn't need to separate myself from her emotionally even thought we were apart physically.

a wave of relief

And I had experienced immediate, wondrous proof of the power of Zen meditation. . .

I was beginning to feel prepared for anything.

The months slipped by quickly at the Zen Center. Nearly six months passed... Sometimes I wondered what on earth I was doing there; other times I knew what I was doing there.

time passes...

Finally, it was time to leave — it came in the form of a very clear message from the Universe: The administrator and his right-hand man called me into their office one morning and said that they knew that I had been smoking grass and, worse yet, that I had slept with a girl who had come there for other reasons... They seemed quite upset about it all, and asked me to leave for a week, and then to come back, after the girl had left.

time to leave

I found my Zen training to come in very handily at this time — I know I would have felt hurt, resentful, uptight, defensive, and probably self-righteous in a similar situation a year or two before that... But I felt very calm, relaxed, looking at their words as a message from the Universe that it was time to flow on. I could see their point of view. They were just doing what they felt was right.

I thanked them for sharing their feelings, and apologized if I caused any trouble, and left immediately — but not before saying goodbye to Mr. Sekida, who smiled so sweetly, like a little baby...

saying goodbye

Maui

an island's secrets

THE ISLAND OF MAUI called me: there were many secrets to be discovered in its forests, beaches, oceans, craters, lava flows, people. The true Hawaiians have long since been nearly destroyed, first by England, then by America. Almost all the fertile areas of Maui are owned by a huge corporation called 'A and B, Inc.' — standing for Alexander and Baldwin, the first two 'Christian' missionaries on the island, who, while supposedly introducing the teachings of Christ, also managed to take control of the island and make themselves and their descendants super-rich. I question this modern interpretation of Christianity. As a result, there is much political unrest in Hawaii. Yet there is also incredible beauty and magic.

I walked all over the island, stopping now and then to just sit quietly, and do nothing. . . feeling the energizing effects of Zen meditation, feeling strong and clear.

Zen training is excellent for Westerners' minds — it immediately cuts thru rational thinking. . . You just sit there. . . and let thoughts go. . . and *be*. . . And suddenly, you discover a powerful source of strength and insight.

I kept thinking of Mr. Sekida's words — words like

> *Just watch a tree growing. . . that is the teaching of Zen*

ocean and sun and stars

I wandered back to Makena Beach — it was seven miles off a paved road, difficult to reach, and many people were living there, freely. . . I lived there for several months, on and off, communing with the ocean and the sun and the stars. . .

Evenings were usually spent around a fire, where people would gather, music would be played, food shared and enjoyed, sometimes with wine, sometimes with grass or hash. . . Sometimes the music would become incredibly intense and deep, and everyone would feel it, and there would be beautiful group singing and dancing.

and singing and dancing

People would go up to the crater — 10,000 feet above the ocean (the highest mountains in the world, if you measure them from the ocean floor) for full moon celebrations. Descriptions of that space and time are beyond words. . .

Maui was for me a place of incredible energy and growth. From Minneapolis to Berkeley to Maui was in a way a journey from one level of consciousness to another to another, each progressively higher and clearer and more open. For awhile, I thought that I would just meditate — that is enough, that's all that is necessary to do.

a journey

into meditation

I still think that that's true, but my understanding of what 'meditation' is has expanded a great deal since then. . . Meditation is every moment. . . it is being calm and clear. . . it is the skillful means to accomplish everything that needs to be done.

I had met a girl named Leilani Lewis while I was at the Youth Congress in Honolulu. . . She told me she owned three acres of land on Maui, high up on the central crater, with an old barn on it. She said I was welcome to stay there at any time.

I went there, first with a beautiful, spunky lady I had met on Makena Beach. And then I went back there, alone. I didn't know why, and I wondered why, but I was clearly getting the message that I should go live there alone for awhile. I started realizing more clearly that all along, I have been following an inner voice which is always showing me the best thing to do next. . . But at times, it just didn't seem to make any sense. . . I could have very comfortably and happily stayed with that beautiful lady, but I knew I had to go off alone — though I was sorry to leave her, and part of me was asking why. . . Why live alone, when you can live with a beautiful companion? But the time had come to live alone.

being alone

an inner voice

As I look back on those days alone, I can see that they were some of the deepest and most rewarding of my life. . .

81

Paradise

I didn't do too much — got up when I felt like it, ate quite a bit, watered some special plants I was cultivating, read, wrote, played my guitar, sang, and just hung out a lot, watching the clouds dance across the top of the crater. . .

After a few days, I was listening more clearly to that inner voice. . . The words that come from within are always clear, simple, sensible. . . They tell me exactly what to do — when to move, when to relax. . . Connecting with this inner voice led me to a place of deep relaxation, where I recharged psychic batteries. . . I felt refreshed, strengthened in a new and different way. I felt there were infinite possibilities in front of me. I felt my search was beginning to be rewarded, in many deep and unexpected ways. . .

I woke up one morning and heard these words in my head (very clearly — because I hadn't talked to anyone in days. . .) — "This is the day to get ready to leave." So I packed up my stuff and came walking down the mountain. It took me all day to walk about eight miles. I lingered everywhere, just hanging out, playing music to myself and the trees, and drinking deeply of the incredible beauty of that island. God, it is PARADISE!

I felt refreshed, strengthened in a new and different way. . . I felt there were infinite possibilities in front of me. . . I felt my search was beginning to be rewarded, in many deep and unexpected ways. . .

That morning I saw four rainbows. . .

And that afternoon, I saw a jet plane flying east, and I knew it was time to move on.

I feel content, yet unborn,
Like a silent new Moon,
While Mother Nature so sweetly
Sings her tune

Gypsy life —
Northern California

CAROL HAD gotten some money from the sale of a small house that Marlow had given her in Minneapolis, and she was determined to get it into land. She went to Minnesota, and, spontaneously, a whole caravan was formed, which included many old friends from earlier, different times. . . I had planned to meet them in northern California, near the coast, near a place called Whitethorn.

So I scrounged an air fare (I was into scrounging at that time) and flew to San Francisco, then hitched to Whitethorn. They weren't there yet, so I wandered the hills, mostly alone, for a few days, camping out, under the stars.

One day there was a large community feast — I spent nearly the entire day in a big sauna, running out every now and then to dive into a cool country brook. When I went into the sauna for the first time, I thought it was totally empty. Then I noticed a strange, vague shape huddled in the corner, on the highest bench, near the ceiling. As my eyes got used to the dark, I could see what looked like a beautiful, wild forest creature, like a piece of sculpture. Then I recognized that it was Jeremy! — a very gentle, lithe soul I had met before in Berkeley. He had transformed: he had rolled in the mud, so that he was completely caked with it — no skin was visible at all, nothing but clay. Even his long tangled hair was a solid piece of clay. He looked like he was out of another time, another place.

Jeremy was a dancer. He had built a tiny, fairytale hut deep in the forest, near a friend who had a large expanse of floor. He would often dance there. And at community gatherings, he would do spontaneous dance-theater, often using some strange kind of forest costume or wild makeup. He once showed me his collection of photographs of different events, different costumes. He was a one-man theater company. And he knew some of the magic of the forests. He would spend much time in the woods, listening. . .

Carol
& a caravan

a feast,
a sauna,

& Jeremy,
forest dancer

83

a light, lovely day

We teamed together for the day. Everyone who came into the sauna found some kind of spacy activity going on. I played my harp (harmonica) while everyone moved, danced. . . we got into group massage — foot massage especially. . . and we told group stories, with everyone contributing. It was a light, lovely day. . .

After nearly a week of waiting, I began to think that maybe they hadn't been able to leave Minnesota yet, so I started out hitching back to Minnesota. I got as far as Arcata — close to the Oregon border — and suddenly I had a strong impulse to turn back. So I just crossed the road and headed back. As I was walking back into Whitethorn, I saw a schoolbus with Minnesota plates coming up the road — and it was them! — just coming in from Minnesota. Carol was there, looking beautiful — looking like a gypsy, with an exquisite silk scarf. And Danny Campbell was with them, too, which was a big surprise. It was so good to see so many old friends together. . .

friends arrive

We wandered around for weeks, living like gypsies, camping anywhere we could, looking for land, not finding anything that was right for us. We saw several pieces of formerly beautiful land which was now a waste land — it had been logged heavily — parts were clear-cut. . . and it was filled with piles of 'slash' everywhere — all the branches and other 'unuseable' parts of the trees. . .

I remember coming across a bare, dried up field, filled with massive redwood stumps. I suddenly realized that it had been, not too long ago, a lush, cool grove of huge trees. My eyes filled with tears. What have we done to our Mother Earth?

caravan

Another bus from Minnesota joined us. Then another. Then a Ford Econoline, which had the irritating habit of breaking down every 60 miles or so, and then an old Studebaker. . . We had grown to become a fairly large caravan, twenty people or so. . .

gypsies

A book fell into our hands, and everybody read it and treasured it. It affected the whole group's consciousness and lifestyle. It was called *The Gypsies* by Jan Yoors — a beautifully poetic account of Romany life written by a young German who had run away at the age of 12 to join the gypsies, and lived with them for 10 years. . .

The book cut thru so many potential worries and hassles — it made us fully appreciate the here and now, the wandering itself, rather than getting into the trap of thinking we needed something else, like land, like a home, like warmth and security, whatever, before we could be happy. There is a wealth of simple, practical, and deep wisdom and insight in gypsy 'philosophy' and living styles. . . Let the gypsies be reborn again!

Let the Gypsies be reborn again

Later, I wrote a poem, remembering these days, and the books I had read and stories I had heard. . .

>Let the Gypsies be reborn!
>   Let them wander again
>Thru fields of green grass
>   Selling amulets and fennel —
>
>Herbs picked from green fields,
>   From forests and deserts
>Oils pressed from flowers
>   Charms for health and weather
>
>Charms for prosperity
>   Charms for your lover
>Cures for your sickness
>   Cures for your Mother. . .
>
>Healing a blind child!
>   It's true! — Working wonders
>Throwing cares to the wind
>   Living in the moment's wonder
>
>Knowing just when to die
>   Being strong til that moment
>Tying up all affairs
>   Calmly awaiting the moment
>
>When you're free at last
>   Of this physical body
>Sailing into Eternity
>   Sailing into new Life
>
>Let the Gypsies be reborn!
>   Let them wander again. . .
>Thru fields of green grass
>   Selling amulets and fennel. . .

We camped in the open fields, and in the woods by a river, and on an old ranch, and right by the ocean, staying for a few days, exploring the area, and moving on. . .

babes in the woods

One day while camping at an old ranch, the older kids — four girls all around 11 years old and one boy, 9 — announced they were going to perform a play that evening, with a surprise ending. Two of the kids were Carol's — Gwynneth and Charlie — and they often used to do improvisational plays and gymnastic events and circuses of strange sorts. They marked out a playing area and got all the set pieces together — tables and chairs. And they dragged two of the women from the audience, because they needed somebody to play their mothers. . .

a Kid's Lib play

The play was hilarious. It began in the house of the uptight, worried mother, who wouldn't let the kids do anything, wanted them in bed early, and so on — *"because I'm your mother."* So the kids rebel and leave, and go to the house of the hip mother, who lets them have their freedom. It was a Kids Lib play.

with a big climax

They had said earlier, with many giggles, that there was going to be a big climax, a shocking ending, to the piece. The ending was a wild celebration, where the kids were dancing around and around, joyfully playing in the house of their newly adopted mother. . . suddenly one of the girls (after several of them had whispered to her, 'Do it! Do it!') moved down center, lifted her long skirts and joyfully and blatantly pissed on the ground. . . It was an amazing touch — beautiful and hilarious. . . Then they all went running off wildly, and disappeared into the woods, telling us to play some music. . .

I hadn't enjoyed a play that much in years. The kids were a constant source of life energy and be-here-now excitement. . . And the four girls were all very lovely — each one a beauty, dressed like gypsy girls. . .

There were such nights around the campfire! Music, even dancing when the music soared. . . singing in 4-part harmonies, 12-part harmonies. . . Music is magic. Music is meditation.

music

Morning yoga, too, became a group activity that many participated in — yet it was very open and freeform, each doing their own. . . The music and the yoga and the wandering and the gypsy life fused a deep bond. . .

& yoga

We definitely had our ups and downs, of course, individually and collectively.

ups & downs

One grey day, we were camped right on a beach in northern California. It was cold and foggy, and we were wet and cranky and running out of money. We were stuck there while vehicles were being repaired — the old Econoline for the seventeenth time. . . We just sat around the fire — it was too cold to do anything else — and ate a long breakfast. There was nothing to do but eat and drink coffee. . . After breakfast we started right in on making lunch. . .

All the children had disappeared. So had Barbara Neill — Barbara had joined us in California, bringing rays of sunshine and her own special magic with her. . . Suddenly, I heard laughing and shouting: I looked up from my depression and saw a beautiful sight — I'll never forget it — it lifted my spirits immediately, and made me want to laugh and sing: Barbara and all the children, of all ages, were holding hands, naked, running down the beach, laughing and dancing as if the fog and the cold didn't matter a bit. . .

rays of sunshine

Suddenly, the day transformed. . .

Creative anarchy: Southern Oregon

WE FINALLY FOUND LAND in southern Oregon, near the coast. It was already September, and winter was coming soon. The old Ford Econoline van broke down regularly every 60 miles on the way up to Oregon, but we'd repair it with paper clips, rubber bands, and chewing gum, and keep on truckin'. . .

A girl named Franny and her husband John or 'JTR', both from Minnesota, had joined us in northern California. Franny was very special, very beautiful. She was over seven months pregnant when we met them. A few days after we arrived in Oregon, she had her baby. . . The birth was a beautiful ritual. Unforgettable. I became amazed at the power of a woman's instincts. Carol was the midwife. Franny was only 17, yet she knew exactly what she needed, and she was completely aware, deeply centered. . . The birth was accompanied by music and chanting. It was a meditation on the forces of life. . .

birth

Franny

Franny is one of the freest, most relaxed and conscious mothers I have even known. She has much to teach. She is into herbs, gardening, art (a very skilled visual artist), Eastern thought, yoga. . .

gypsy skills

Everyone got into such amazingly diverse things in the country. . . it was 'creative anarchy' — a phrase we often used, a phrase which everyone defined differently. Thoreau would have loved it. . . There were no leaders, per se — and yet everyone was a leader in some way. The leaders for each individual project emerged spontaneously, depending on who had the greatest knowledge or experience. . .

The group included Michael Simon and Terry Crab, living wildly, hunting and fishing, building their log cabin in the woods. . . and 'Magic Matthew', the group's Capricorn, getting into what he felt were two of the dirtiest and most essential occupations: plumbing and politics. . . and beautiful Moonchild sister Barbara Neill, with her incredibly wondrous hand-made tapestries, very successful at the fairs, so beautiful and gentle, so loved by all the children. . . and

Liza and her herbal healing. . . and Michael Biezants and his mandolin, his well-kept bus and his beautiful lady Joy. . . and Gino, a former child actor from New York City, building a dome, planting the garden, cooking Italian feasts, eventually getting into running a sandwich shop in Coos Bay. . . and there was Sarah, getting into nursing. . . and John Berman and Steve, getting into building. . . and Carol transforming into a gypsy and a yogi, and getting into gardening. . . so many free spirits. . . so much growth and change. . .

all kinds of people

Carol and I did yoga every morning, then worked a fairly full day, mostly building, trying to get enough warm and dry space for the winter. Evenings were usually filled with music, with some of the *Lord of the Rings* read later on. . . By November, we had our central area finished, and had a large, crowded, happy house-warming party, with music, dancing, food, home-made wine. . . We had thought we were moving into the middle of Nowhere — I didn't think there was anyone around who would come to that party. . . I'll bet over a hundred people showed up, all living within a radius of 20 or 30 miles. . . all kinds of people — people I really grew to love. . .

I began to read a lot, in the country, as winter set in. . . I slowly read all the writings of Mahatma Gandhi that I could find. Like Thoreau (who influenced Gandhi!), he says so much that is relevant to today's world in such a simple and brilliant way. . .

a tribute to Gandhi

Gandhi's energy was powerful enough to change the world. . . to overcome so much injustice. . . to overthrow what was at that time the world's most powerful government. He blended the political and the social and the spiritual, perhaps like no other person in history. . . Attempts to live our lives and to run our governments by exercising so many forms of violence over other individuals have not been effective in creating their desired ends. Violence only breeds more violence. Gandhi grew to understand this, and taught this, and lived this. Unconditional love — open acceptance of all humankind, even though you may disagree with the games they're playing — can't lose, because it will never breed any resistance.

& Thoreau

And I read Thoreau, beautifully relevant today.

> Do we call this the land of the free?
> What is it to be free from King George and continue the slaves of King Prejudice?
> What is it to be born free and not to live free?
> What is the value of any political freedom, but as a means to moral freedom?
> We tax ourselves unjustly.
> We quarter troops, we quarter fools. . .
> We quarter our gross bodies on our poor souls, till the former eat up all the latter's substance.
> It is our children's children who may perchance be really free.
> —Henry David Thoreau

Henry David, I pray that your words are coming true. . .

meeting a magical being

During this time, I had a little tent to myself deep in the woods. One morning, I stuck my head out of the tent, and found myself looking directly, deeply, into the eyes of a huge, magnificent buck. . . He looked at me openly, quietly, deeply, not moving. . . he was the king of the forest, with a strong, beautiful chest, standing proud and graceful. He was unafraid. I was in awe. He was so exquisite, crowned with magnificent antlers. . . Then he slowly turned, and leapt away, seeming to fly over the dense brush, an entrancing forest dancer. He was a magical being — there was no questioning that. And he had given me a beautiful blessing. . .

ducks

& hunters

One morning I spent many hours watching flocks of ducks fly into a lake that had just been a field, but was now filled with early winter rains. I saw hundreds of ducks flying in, resting for a moment on their long journey, eating, playing, squawking. . . I went back up to the road and soon met three hunters with ominous looking rifles over their shoulders. They asked me if I had seen any ducks, and I said no, I hadn't seen a duck in weeks. . . the hunting has been terrible around here this year. . .

I had a long phone conversation with my brother Will in Minnesota. He said the folks had gone thru some good changes. Then he told me a story — one which deeply moved me:

& my folks

My father had gone on a big hunting expedition with a group of executives from his company, including his boss... Dad had always been a hunter, and even a trap shooter — shooting clay 'traps' for sport... There were trophies and a big gun rack on the basement wall...

a hunting story

A group of them had flown from Minnesota to Montana, deep into the Rocky Mountains. They were given high-powered rifles with high powered scopes...

My father sighted a Rocky Mountain Bighorn ram at a great distance — 300 yards or something — thru his scope. He fired a single shot, and the animal dropped instantly... He walked over to it... As he approached, that beautiful ram raised his head and looked my father deeply into his eyes — as if he was in anguish, as if he was asking *"Why?"*

Then the ram dropped dead.

My father dropped his rifle, and left. Other people in his party eventually carried the ram and his rifle out — he wouldn't touch either one. And he hasn't touched a rifle since.

I was deeply touched by my brother's story. I even started to feel that perhaps there's some hope for the older generation after all...

hope for the older generation

A little later, my father sent me a letter — and the tone of it was very different from before, in earlier days: he was warm and open and friendly. He even quoted Thoreau — one of the most beautiful things he ever wrote, I feel —

> "If a man does not keep pace with his companions, perhaps it is because he hears a different drummer. Let him step to the music which he hears, however measured or far away."

My father had made a clear and welcomed move towards reconciliation with that letter. It was a statement of acceptance — and it was the beginning of the end of several years of separation. It felt like a weight had been lifted. I wrote them back, and we started communicating once again.

communicating once again

L IKE GYPSIES, we were finding all kinds of crafts and work and scams to allow us to survive in the world, in comfort, and yet to be our own masters, completely... Free will, individualism was encouraged: it truly was creative anarchy. Christmas was drawing near. Almost all of us got into making candles. Magic Matthew earned his name here, because he got into making incredibly detailed, wondrous landscape sculptures: a medieval castle on a hill, surrounded by a mote... mountains and rivers... a volcano with flowing lava of hot wax... We sold the candles and other things on the streets in Coos Bay — it was a good scam, we made several hundred dollars, and we played music to pass the time. Crowds gathered. Some of the songs just took off on their own, the energy affecting everyone. We sang Bob Dylan's "The Times They Are A-Changing" to a large group of people, mostly open kids, worried mothers, spirited friends, and uncomprehending policemen... These words were especially meaningful:

Christmas candles

changin times in Coos Bay

> Come Mothers and Fathers thruout the land
> And don't criticize what you can't understand
> Your sons and your daughters are beyond your command
> The old order is rapidly changing...
>
> (Bob Dylan)

I was still in theater, in spite of myself.

Then came a very strange, unexpected form of theater:

One afternoon, two cars drove up, filled with very friendly, smiling, energetic straight people... They introduced themselves and brought beer, which made them very welcome. We were glad to have such warm and friendly contact with our neighbors. They invited us to a meeting, 40 miles away. We said it was too far to drive. They said they'd pick us up and take us to it. They said there was plenty of coffee and cookies and other goodies. We weren't starving, but we weren't getting fat, either... So, many of us went — some to see what they were into, and some for the food...

friendly neighbors

They were into what they called Buddhism — 'true Buddhism': Nicheran Dishonan Buddhism. Actually, it's not Buddhism at all, because their teachings are not the teachings of Buddha. They claim that Nicheran Dishonan is the 'true Buddha' who surpasses Shakyamuni Buddha. (It's

'Nicheran Dishonan Buddhism'

like somebody calling themselves a Christian, but saying that the true Christ really came later, in the 14th century or so.)

Yet I was impressed, in spite of myself, by their strength and positive, high energy. Their meetings are something like old high school pep fests — cheering, shouting, loud chanting in unison. They literally wind up energy. Much of their power comes from their mantra,

pep fests revisited

nam myoho renge kyo

These words are their magic. They chant them daily, enthusiastically, rubbing their prayer beads like a gambler rubs dice... And it works — it achieves their desires, though their desires seemed to me to be totally materialistic. I actually heard a man say at one of their meetings, "I got my $17,000 trailer house by chanting *nam myoho renge kyo*."

They've become huge and powerful in Japan, apparently — or so the group says. They have mass rallies, with tens of thousands of people, they have tremendous economic resources — all thru chanting *nam myoho renge kyo*. Easy as pie. Their meetings are often big gala events, filled with old-fashioned entertainment: stage bands, dancers, chorus lines, baton twirlers, choirs, talent show stuff — a lot of things that haven't been seen in this country since the early '50s...

Some of us got into it for awhile — mostly because they would drive 40 miles out of their way to pick us up for these meetings (a total of 160 miles for them, going and coming, on country roads). But I was also drawn to it because the mantra does have a lot of power — it obviously gave them a great deal of energy and strength. And it worked for us, too, when we used it...

But our interest soon waned — mostly because it was so weak philosophically and so blatantly materialistic. Besides, we were getting tired of such huge doses of coffee and cookies...

Carol and I decided to leave on New Year's Eve — there wasn't enough warm and dry space for everybody, and our yoga was getting difficult to continue. It had been a very good experience for me — a time to relax and absorb on deeper levels all the things I had been learning. This is a very

deciding to leave

time to let knowledge become experience

necessary part of any kind of education or growth: we need time to reflect, time to digest what we have learned, time to let knowledge become experience.

Yet, Carol and I were both looking for something else, but we knew not what... So we left, amid warm good-byes, to continue our pilgrimage. We were searching for teachings, and visiting holy places — a true pilgrimage, in a sense.

Oregon will always remain a very special place in my heart. The people there have a unique quality about them — they're free, they're individualistic. Many Oregonians are former Oakies, and they have an open accepting spirit... I may go back there one day — who knows?

our pilgrimage continues

We decided to go to San Francisco for starters — about 800 miles away. We got out on the paved road which led to the highway, stuck out our thumbs, and started chanting *'Nam myoho renge kyo . . . nam myoho renge kyo. . .'* Within two minutes, a VW camper pulled up, luxuriously outfitted, and the couple in it said they were going all the way to San Francisco.

It's an amazing mantra, all right...

Pilgrimage to San Francisco

WE STAYED WITH THE FIREHOUSE THEATER people again in San Francisco. I have never lost contact with those people.

The Firehouse

They had gone thru many changes, too — they had lightened up considerably. At that time, they were doing a play of Nancy Walter's called *Blessings* — a whole new direction for the theater, a positive and exhuberant statement. I heard the music, by John Franzen, many times — the music in itself was a blessing. Some of the energy of the production reminded me of the Floating Lotus. . .

lightened up, into Blessings

They all lived together in a large old Victorian house on Gough Street in San Francisco. And they had discovered what I had discovered: communal living is in itself theater. . . The meals, the music, the children, the very special events like marriages and births, the mundane things like drinking beer or smoking dope or washing clothes, relating to each other, the whole texture of life becomes a communal ritual.

communal living

We are consciously seeking for tribal forms once more — which includes living together and discovering group rituals, expressions of togetherness, of unity with each other, and with the earth. . .

discovering group ritual

The day we arrived, the big house was empty. Everyone had gone to the ocean, to perform their own kind of marriage ceremony for Marlow and Brigitte. It was a totally novel kind of ceremony, and it sounded beautiful. When people returned in the evening, the energy was high and joyous. A spontaneous party developed, with much merry-making and music and comedy. . .

a marriage ceremony

My 3rd, and last, letter

And afterwards, I wrote my third, and last, letter to Tony Steblay.

> Late Jan. ('71)
> Sun in Aquarius
> Moon in Aquarius

Dear Tony, A rare letter. . .

I think of you often, often wonder what's happening at your school, theatrically and politically and spiritually. . . has the conservative backlash occurred?. . . Do you have any academic freedom?. . . How is the modular scheduling developing — can the community dig it?

It's so hard for most people to accept change — and yet we're in a sea of change. Such a paradox. . .

more open-minded

I feel more open-minded these days (I think I can truthfully say that), less separated from people, even very different people, like cops and straight housewives and truck drivers. There's change — revolutionary change — happening in their lives too, happening on every level. It doesn't really matter whether we drop out or drop in — it'll all work out anyway.

the caravan

I left Hawaii in August — it was incredibly beautiful there, but I got word from Carol in Georgeville, Minnesota, that she and 12 others were getting a bus ready to drive out to the west coast, in search of land. I met them in northern California. Our number grew to 25 — three school buses, a van, and two funky cars.

Oregon

By early September we had bought and settled on 40 acres in Southwest Oregon, about six miles from the ocean. Climate's pretty moderate, and the land is beautiful. We were able to plant a winter garden, and we built a small, 22-foot diameter geodesic dome, elevated on a cylinder with a bigger diameter — it looks a little like a funky Taj Mahal — it's the warm and dry communal kitchen, living room, shop, etc. We're sleeping around it in tents and lean-to "plastic-panic architecture."

Basic, survival level living — it hasn't been entirely satisfactory. Some things there are very beautiful: livin' in the country, eating good, living simply, making music nearly every night, getting into crafts, getting into the group — some of our meetings and gatherings have been very high, very fine. . . But some things aren't so fine: we're really short of warm and dry space, and certain people's egos are getting in the way of other people's egos, and the group is not together on a spiritual plane — many would rather play cards and drink beer — what a far-out revolution this is!

So, at New Year's, Carol and I left. . . Both of us felt a need for some kind of pilgrimage, some kind of spiritual rejuvenation.

So far our pilgrimage has led only to San Francisco, to the Firehouse mansion. We were thinking of going to Minneapolis, but now some other possibilities have become known to us — one in Baja, and one in New Mexico. . . We're still undecided, as usual — there are so many possibilities. . .

pilgrimage

My interest in Zen seems to be giving way to an interest in Yoga and Tibetan Buddhism — all roads lead to the same awakened state, every master from Christ to Bodhidharma to Suzuki Roshi is saying essentially the same thing. But for every different temperament there's a different path. . .

different paths

Wow — these Aquarian moons really blow my mind, every time, every month. I only talk like this when the moon's in Aquarius — mad ecstatic visions of the New World, mass elevation of consciousness. . . More and more are seeing it, it seems to me. San Francisco and Berkeley are really far-out these days, and the country around here is even more incredible. . .

visions of a New World

I wrote a song — it begins
  I used to have doubts and worries
  Sometimes I'd feel we're so wrong
  But now I know we're on the road to the Revelation —
That's what I have to say in this song. . .

a song

Holly is pregnant — due in July. She and John really wanted to have a baby. She seems really fine these days — high energy — working for the Firehouse, reading, baking. John's music is far-out these days. . . new forms, sometimes classical sounding, sometimes jazz, sometimes hillbilly, but always in a new form. Hard to describe — goes well with the Firehouse insanity.

babies and music

Their last play, *Blessings*, was beautiful — a real positive celebration, for the most part, of being together. . . But now they're doing Buchner's *Woyzeck* again — do you know the play? Written about 1830, I guess. It seems to me to be mostly about insanity, R.D. Laing mind-fucks, and killing your old lady because she balled another man. All those old games — and lots of grotesque, painful images, the kind of thing Marlow really digs. He's directing it — it's played at such a fever pitch that the actors are really hard on their own bodies. . . It's a painful experience, but with moments of light, moments of beauty, and much audience contact — some of it very effective. They're opening it some time in February, soon. . . They've got a beautiful theater building, near here, in downtown S.F.

Blessings and Woyzeck

Half of the Firehouse group wants to move to the country. They may do it in a year or so — get the plays together in the country and then tour them. Marlow has already bought 60 acres of land in northern California! Remote — an hour and a half walk from the nearest road. . .

Letter (concluded)

I hope all is well with you and yours... May you find joy in your work, in your life...

Carol gives you a warm hello... She's even more beautiful these days than ever before, if you can imagine that...

Take it easy... peace be with you...

...om... shanti... shanti... shanti...
...om... shanti... shanti... shanti...
...om... peace... peace... peace...
...om....Love,
Mark

Victorian funk

The Firehouse house was large and Victorian and amazing. Sometimes people would walk in and their jaws would drop in amazement. Elegant Victorian Funk. Usually in a state of chaos, mostly due to pets and kids.

the pets

The pets were almost as far-out as the kids — Marlow had two crazy monkeys and a large oscelot, who was even crazier. Constant drama. The oscelot (named, appropriately, Shiva) wanted to *eat* those monkeys, and to get out of his cage... One time he did (get out, that is — he never quite managed to eat the monkeys), and he went racing down California Avenue... a woman was walking up the street with a red dress under her arm. Suddenly, a huge ferocious cat leapt on her, tore the red dress from her, and took off down the street with his prey... Police were called, and, with the aid of several squad cars, and a huge amount of paraphernalia, including tranquilizer guns, managed to trap the raging beast... They knew immediately who it belonged to, too — the Firehouse was notorious.

Danny Campbell was back with them at that time, too. He had a beautiful monkey, named Isadora — an incredible spider monkey, with a very small, lithe body and long arms and legs. She was maybe 3 feet tall or more when she stood up... Isadora would make friends with you in the most beautiful way — she was a true charmer. She'd come on very coquettish, flirt with you, and dance in front of you. Then she'd cuddle up to you for an instant — then she'd leap out of your arms and fly around the room — jumping joyfully from the top of the doorsill to a lamp to another doorsill, circling the entire room... she'd come down with a feet-to-feet backflip, and do a few more acrobatic feats, brilliantly, for you. . .

They got into trouble with her too. She would occasionally find an open window, and go leaping across the roofs of the apartment buildings. . . then she'd find an open kitchen window and go in and steal food. She scared a few housewives. . .

And if anyone had any marijuana, she had an uncanny knack of finding it and eating it. She loved dope. . . she was a true freak at heart. The Firehouse was a circus.

The kids in that house were amazing, too. . . Beautiful Nina got into ballet when she was about eight, and her life became one total, endless dance — simply walking was much too boring. Lily is just as beautiful as Nina (Lionhearted Lily is a super-Leo, Nina is an Aries — two strong, fiery signs). Lily and I used to hang out together at times. Sometimes she would give me trouble, sometimes she would give me teachings. One day, we were crawling thru the attic, and she found something on the floor, and grabbed it with great energy and wonder. She clasped her fist around it, so I couldn't see it, and held it in front of me. "Oh! This is magic!" she said, "Most people don't know it's magic, and so it doesn't have any power for them. But I know that this is magic." Then she opened her hand. She was holding a cat's eye marble. . .

the kids

Later, one time, she got very sad and misty-eyed and said, "I know when I grow up, I'm gonna lose my magic — I can feel it. . . I don't want to grow up and lose all my magic!". . .

from the mouths of babes

Lily was six years old, then. . .

Our pilgrimage continued. I roamed around the City, checking out every place listed under 'Yoga' in the Yellow Pages. . . There is an incredible variety of spiritual activity going on in the Bay Area. . .

I went to the Integral Yoga Institute — founded by Swami Satchidananda. It seemed lovely, but lightweight.

Integral Yoga,

Carol and I both took a few Kundalini Yoga classes, too, but it seemed too physically strenuous and jarring, and the people in the trip were imitating so many things that seemed to me to be merely superficial — like turbins and white yoga clothes. . .

and Kundalini Yoga

To each their own — but that trip was not for me.

Steve Gaskin

Steve Gaskin arrived back in town at that time. He had just returned from a trip around the entire country in a huge caravan, with dozens of buses. . .

Carol and I went to see him talk in a misty-morning park right near the ocean cliffs, a Sunday morning in Sutro Park. There were dozens of buses parked everywhere. Most of them were marked with a blue mandala, a symbol of their unity.

Stephen talked — saying that he realized during this trip around the country that what they were doing was in some ways very new, unique, at least in terms of recent American history. Now he felt that he just couldn't go back to the old form of his Monday night classes in the City — he had decided to head east to look for land, and anyone interested was invited to join him. It came as a big surprise to almost everybody. He said he wanted to leave very soon, that week. . . Most of the people who had been on the caravan went with him. They later found a large chunk of land in Tennessee, and it has grown still larger. . . Stephen is a fine teacher, with a lot of innovative ideas — like the funky, gut-level metaphors he uses when interpreting spiritual material, and like group marriages. I watch that group with interest.

Alan Watts

Alan Watts was very popular and very conspicuous around there, too, at that time — I saw and heard him many times, and read many of his books. I think Watts was a genius in interpreting the East for the West. I don't mean to use the word genius lightly — he was unquestionably brilliant. He wrote *The Way of Zen* (or was it *The Spirit of Zen*?) when he was only 19 years old — and that book has a very clear understanding of Zen, something which, like Tibetan Buddhism, has been so often grossly misunderstood and misinterpreted.

'a spiritual entertainer'

Watts was very theatrical — robes, beard, wine, women. . . he called himself a 'spiritual entertainer', and he was a master of spontaneous, light-hearted theatrics. I feel that this is one of the side-products, one of the results, of a real meaningful search for truth. It's no accident that so many of the Zen stories center on unique, spontaneous, almost childlike behavior — once Zen is understood, a person is free to express themselves in an infinite variety of ways.

Altamont

AN AMAZING PIECE OF THEATER happened around this time, of a scope and power that this world had never seen before: the Altamont Rock Concert.

Talk on the streets went wild one day — the Rolling Stones were giving a free concert, along with the Grateful Dead, Jefferson Airplane, Santana (my favorite group at that time) and several other groups. . . I couldn't pass up the chance to hear some of the world's greatest rock 'n roll. . . The Beatles had broken up, and the Stones were unquestionably the biggest and baddest group in the world.

I arrived there the night before, like a great many others. Hitching there was easy, because about every third car heading east out of Berkeley was going there. . . It was to be held in a large area of rolling meadows next to a Speedway, where they usually hold those insane stock car races. Thousands of people were already there. They scattered out over the hills. Almost everyone joined a campfire, or made their own — there was plenty of wood, most of it ripped off (literally) from a long, winding slat fence that was put up in a vain attempt to section off part of the meadows. As it grew dark, the hills in the distance were dotted with a thousand fires — it looked fantastical — and there was music, and good times. . .

That first night was beautiful. People were very friendly, mellow. . . they were saying it was another Woodstock, which was a wonderful experience for nearly everyone. I played music, and met some very beautiful people there that night. Including a lovely lady from Hawaii, who was now living in Santa Cruz. There was a warm tribal feeling — people would wander freely from campfire to campfire, saying hello, rapping, sharing wine and food and whatever they had. 'Twas a lovely night.

But the next day, things started getting strange. A lot of it had to do with the sheer masses of people — estimated at 500,000, a countless number, actually. I sat fairly close to the

Altamont: the Rolling Stones' free concert

'Twas a lovely night. . . but the next day. . .

an ant-like mass of bodies

stage, and could see, above and behind the stage, a solid mass of people in a long line moving slowly toward the stage. It looked strange and stark, like the last image of Bergman's *The Seventh Seal* — a solid mass of people in the foreground, then the stage, then above and behind it (you could see quite a distance — the perspective looked like a medieval painting) bare, vacant hills which were crowned at the very top with a dense, slowly moving, endlessly patient, ant-like mass of bodies. . . The line continued, unbroken, all day, and in some ways became a deep part of the whole experience. In the morning, they were all moving together, coming in. By early afternoon, it was moving in both directions simultaneously, as some people started leaving. By late afternoon, the direction had completely shifted, and everyone was leaving. A great many left way before the Stones even played. . .

a problem of space

There was a problem of space. People were sitting as close together as physically possible, and they were continually being packed tighter as more people came. By midmorning, it was such a dense ocean of bodies that it was really difficult, almost impossible, to move thru it, and very few people tried. If you felt you had to move, or urinate or something, it was just too bad, because, in every direction, there was no free space. It started to get intense.

everyone was high

I remember it so clearly. Everyone was high. You needed no alcohol or drugs to get high, although there was plenty around. . . It was in the air, and everyone felt it. Everyone was high on the same energy, high on the music, high on the people. Rock 'n roll is powerful music.

good music: Santana

I can define good music this way: good music is happening when you get goosebumps . . . when you physically feel the thrill, when your spirit soars. Santana was the first group to play, at about 10 a.m. or so. And they played very good music. Goosebumps and soaring spirit. . . powerful, explosive, richly beautiful sounds. . . They were the best group of the whole day, I felt, rivaling the Stones. . .

It all started off so positively and so strongly. . .

After them, there were a few other groups, who were pretty good, but didn't generate the energy that Santana did. Then the Jefferson Airplane (now called Jefferson Starship) came on. They had really helped to start it all, with their 'Jet Age Sound', the San Francisco sound. . . But before they played, there was a weird moment: somebody grabbed a mike and said, loudly, distorting the sound of his voice, "Angel initiates, on stage! Angel initiates on stage!" There were a lot of people on stage, a lot of confusion — it was impossible to maintain order or a clear stage with such an incredibly huge number of bodies packed so closely together. . . Then a biker, a Hell's Angel, came riding thru the crowd. It was nearly impossible to even walk thru that crowd, much less ride a motorcycle thru it. But he did it. It really irritated the people, because they had to almost crush each other to avoid getting run over by this egomaniac's machine. . .

the Airplane & the Angel initiates

The Airplane started playing. They started getting it on, but they didn't have the solid sound of Santana, or the Stones, or of their own albums. Something was happening which was distracting the musicians, and their sound just wasn't together.

Suddenly, abruptly, the music stopped. . . The effect was very weird — the music sets up a certain rhythm, and that rhythm is never just abruptly stopped in a concert situation. It was a shock. Suddenly all the sound stopped, and there was some kind of fight going on, on stage. Then one of the Airplane members, obviously pissed off, yelled into the mike that someone had hit their singer Marty Balen in the mouth.

suddenly, it all stopped

People were getting very irritated with the Angels for their childish, macho, screwed-up behavior — so much of the Angel mentality is an unfortunate hangover from the '50s, the Beat and Lost generation's neuroses. . . I think that Altamont is one of the main things that destroyed the Hell's Angels, because the Angels managed to really offend everybody. Before Altamont, it had been somewhat acceptable to most people to be a biker. They were even kind of folk heroes, in their own way. Rebels with a million causes. They were the Grateful Dead's bodyguards, maintaining order at the larger rock concerts, at least before Altamont — and that was what you could call a respectable position. But they blew it, totally, at Altamont. There was simply no room for their lifestyle in that crowded space.

instant history

The whole event was being filmed — the moviemakers commanded a tower in the middle of this mass of people — and everyone was aware of it. It was instant history.

a strange, surreal day

The Airplane managed to start playing again. Things would quiet down, and then flare up again, and the music would stop again. It went on all afternoon, while several groups attempted to play. The day started to feel interminably long and very strange, surreal. . . Part of it was the effect of the music — several hours of loud rock 'n roll has a definite physiological effect — after five or six hours, it started feeling like an overdose of intense volume. . . and it continued for what seemed like many, many more hours. . . It was too much. And part of it was the huge mass of people, and the contact high. Part of it was the tension of the possibility of violence from those crazy, stoned bikers. . . It was a long, long day. . .

I never thought of leaving, though — it would have been much too much of a hassle getting thru the crowd. . . and I was fascinated, stoned, by the electric energy in the air.

Finally, it began to get dark. The helicopter that had been flying the groups in arrived again, landing behind the stage. But this time it was different — that helicopter was charged with energy. Everyone knew, everyone could tangibly feel, that the Rolling Stones had arrived.

the whole thing was a reflection of the Stones' music. . .

Part of what followed was a huge reflection of the Stone's music. The Beatles were children of light; the Stones were playing with darker forces — with albums like 'His Satanic Majesty's Request' — and some of those forces emerged at Altamont.

It seemed to me as if both the Stones and the Angels were playing with forces they really didn't understand. No one could comprehend or control the forces at play at Altamont — their magnitude was beyond anyone's power to control.

It was completely dark by the time the Stones played. Huge, intense spotlights came on. They suddenly appeared, Mick Jagger and Keith Richards standing together downstage, very powerful. I noticed that the five Stones were in a pentagonal position — the formation that many magicians use. . .

Their music exploded, soaring immediately to incredible heights. They are technically masters of modern music — able to forge one rich, ever changing, pulsating fabric of sound that is explosive beyond words. . . Their first song was 'Jumpin' Jack Flash' — Jagger *is* Jumpin' Jack Flash. . . As their music soared, all I could see was a huge wave of densely packed bodies sweeping onto the stage. Like a tidal wave. Several times, the music stopped. Several times, Mick Jagger pleaded, in a strong but surprisingly sweet and innocent and young-sounding voice, "Brothers and sisters! Cool out, just cool out. . ." And the wave would subside, for awhile. But then they would explode into that powerful music again. And not even Mick Jagger could control that audience. Each time the music stopped it was as if something very ominous was happening. The Stones were threatening to just quit playing. The air was charged. Then (of all things to sing!) they blasted into 'Gimme Shelter' — one of their ultra-heavy numbers —

explosive music

> Rape, murder
> It's just a shot away,
> It's just a shot away —

The energy went wild. I was almost sure that some crazy stoned weirdo was going to shoot Jagger. It was all an incredible movie, anyway. A huge wave of bodies swept onto the stage. It looked like people could be getting crushed. . .

wild energy, waves of bodies

That's all I could see — one dense mass of bodies. Someone was knifed and killed, they say. But we couldn't see it. I guess they got it on film, though. . . What a movie!

The Stones managed to play a fairly short, but incredibly heavy set. Then they disappeared quickly. The Grateful Dead was going to play after them, but they didn't. It would have been impossible — the energy was too explosive, too out of control.

And suddenly, it was all over. It quieted way down, very quickly, as the bright lights went out, and people slowly, patiently, filed out. . .

suddenly, it was over

a dying dark age, a dawning age of light

I did much thinking about Altamont afterwards. Rock 'n roll is a huge mirror which reflects our entire society in all its strengths and weaknesses, darkness and light. It's like the mirror of astrology — the dying, dark Piscean age, and a tiny glimpse of the dawning Aquarian age were writ large for the world to see at Altamont. . .

Chogyam Trungpa, Rinpoche

Chogyam Trungpa & Suzuki Roshi: a study in contrasts

I went with Carol to see Chogyam Trungpa, Rinpoche — one of the youngest and most well-known Tibetan teachers in America. He was speaking at the San Francisco Zen Center.

It was a beautiful scene — a study in contrasts. The Zen Center was so quiet, so sedate, so Japanese — no smoking, no shoes, no loud talking, very clean and simple and orderly.

Trungpa was scheduled to speak at 8:00, and Suzuki Roshi, the founder and master of the Zen Center, was there a few minutes early. He sat up front, but off to one side, in a big, comfortable stuffed chair. He sat down, cross-legged, and immediately went into meditation, without saying a word.

A half an hour passed. Trungpa hadn't shown up yet. Suzuki Roshi just sat there, motionless, totally contented, unconcerned whether anything happened or not.

About 45 minutes passed — then there was an intense burst of noisy energy in the back of the hall. . . Trungpa Rinpoche came in, being supported by someone and not walking too steadily. He had been in a car accident in Europe many months before, and his body looked in pretty bad shape. He looked half drunk, too. . .

Suzuki Roshi opened his eyes. Trungpa greeted him very affectionately — it was touching to see the two together — the old Japanese man with the shaved head and Zen simplicity, and the young Tibetan with his wild shock of hair and Western mannerisms.

Trungpa sat down, front and center, lit up a cigarette and popped open a 16-oz. can of Colt 45. . . Suddenly, things started getting really loose — what had been a formal Zen sitting started turning into a party.

Trungpa started talking, in his high-pitched, beautifully precise Oxford English. . . He talked for about a half hour, chain-smoking, and drinking *three* of those 16-oz. cans of strong beer. . . Carol pointed out that he smoked like a kid who's trying to learn to smoke — and it seemed true!

Suzuki Roshi never said one word. Several times though, he cracked up at something Trungpa said — then Trungpa would crack up, and the two would laugh together. It was very touching.

Carol's attention was riveted upon Trungpa. He really spoke to her. . .

After the short talk, people started asking questions. Things had gotten more relaxed than ever — people were lying all over the floor. . . Someone asked Trungpa this question: "Rinpoche, what do you see?" Trungpa paused long enough to survey the whole large room, and then he answered, nonchalantly, "Chaos. . ."

Trungpa is fantastic at shattering models of what it is to be a spiritual teacher.

I really enjoyed, I must admit, seeing so many short-haired, strict Zen students light up cigarettes afterwards, and smoke — looking a little like rebellious kids. . . in their own way, honoring Trungpa.

silence

& a burst of noisy energy

affectionate greetings

Suzuki Roshi

A Zen master

I SAW SUZUKI ROSHI many times — he was a great teacher of Zen, and he built the San Francisco Zen Center and Tassajara. . . He was very childlike in many ways — very spontaneous and light. . . I loved his sense of humor. . .

One time he was talking about *koans* — the short little Zen sayings and stories that one of the two main schools of Zen, the Rinzai, uses to meditate upon. . . Suzuki Roshi said, "A good koan for Americans is —

'How do I attain enlightenment while driving on the freeway?' "

I went to his funeral, too. It was exquisite — quiet, full of dignity, full of love. Trungpa was there. . . He spoke, and said Suzuki Roshi was like a father to him. It was so beautiful to see a young Tibetan master paying such tribute to an old Japanese master. . . It shattered many boundaries. . .

Break all barriers down
   we have bridges to mend
And a love to lighten
   our laughter
And a love to grow
   everafter

Suzuki Roshi — you are blessed, because you blessed so many others. . .

Tarthang Tulku

SYD WALTER told me he had visited a Tibetan *lama*, or teacher, with the strange name of Tarthang Tulku Rinpoche, who had recently arrived in Berkeley... Syd said it was a very strange and disconcerting experience, because the lama seemed totally bored and disinterested with everything Syd had shared with him. I found this very intriguing, for some reason, and called the 'Tibetan Nyingma Meditation Center'. A man with the strangest accent I had ever heard answered the phone, and I made an appointment to see him.

Three strange things

Our first meeting was brief, but interesting. I hitchhiked from San Francisco to Berkeley. On the way, the guy who picked me up shared two or three joints of his home-grown marijuana with me. It was excellent — nearly as good as Hawaiian grass. I then went in to meet the lama. He was sitting cross-legged, a blanket wrapped around his legs, in a room filled with hundreds of pictures, papers, ritual objects.

our first brief encounter

He took one look at me and said, "I don't think you should smoke that marijuana so much."

And I said, "Why not? I feel it's very good for my growth, and my meditation."

And he said, "I don't think so... I don't think so..."

He had piercing, bright eyes, and a warm, contageous chuckle. He seemed to think that our conversation was very funny. He seemed totally different from the man that Syd had described. I was fascinated by him — there was something very light and childlike and yet very powerful and deep about him. He was a person of many moods and many contrasts. I liked him, immediately, even though he was disagreeing with nearly everything I said.

He gave me a bunch of pictures and prints of different Tibetan teachers and deities and prayers... And he told me to come back, if I felt like it, in a few weeks.

eyes & words

Afterwards, his eyes and his words kept coming to mind. I had the feeling that he was a magician, and a heavyweight teacher. I went back, and was eventually invited to take a weekly class from him — though I had to wait a few months before I could begin. This was typical of him: he never seemed to be in a hurry.

soul-searching, and sweet sorrow

Carol decided to leave San Francisco. After much thought and soul-searching, I decided to stay. Every time we separated, it became easier and easier. . . It was our last time together in which we shared a deep, intimate, loving connection, and I think we both sensed it. But we separated without any bitterness, only with a bit of sweet sorrow. We were moving in different directions. The time had come for both of us to discover ourselves.

Carol went on her way, and ended up at the Lama Foundation in the mountains of northern New Mexico.

She wrote me, and invited me to come and visit. And another chapter of this pilgrimage unfolds.

Lama

I HITCHHIKED FROM SAN FRANCISCO to Taos, New Mexico... On the way, I went thru Yosemite, and stayed and camped awhile. It was so good to see the country again, and to sleep in the open meadows, and later, in the open desert of New Mexico... I grew to love the vastness and the beauty of the desert just as much as the ruggedness and grandeur of Yosemite... No wonder that so many prophets and teachers received their visions in the desert...
What a truly beautiful planet we live on...

Thru Yosemite, and into the desert...

I was warmly welcomed at Lama, and it was warm and special and sweet seeing Carol again. She lived in her own little A-frame house, like most of the other people, snuggled into the woods, away from the two large main buildings — the kitchen/dining room and the central hall/library/baths/kiva building.

Lama — a sacred place

I spent about a month there. In that short time, it felt like I became part of the family. I don't think I have ever absorbed so much in one month, before or since...

Lama is one of the most together and well-organized spiritual communes I've yet seen... Quite a rigorous schedule, though — a little too much for my taste. Everyone got up for a prayer meeting at 6:30 a.m., held in the little round adobe kiva... They were beautiful gatherings — everyone took turns leading them... Then there was breakfast, then physical work — mostly adobe construction — from 8 a.m. to 2 p.m., with a break around 11 for lunch... Then, after 2 p.m., the people who weren't paying to live there worked on one of several crafts projects — making prayer flags, making robes... In the winter they worked on books — *Be Here Now* was done there, and many others.

There was another prayer meeting in the early afternoon, and another before dinner. They were the spiritual glue which kept people together, individually and collectively.

the view from Lama

The view from Lama is fantastic. . . It is 8400 feet up a mountain, and it looks out for miles and miles *and miles* over northern New Mexico, with its beautiful plains and mesas and Rio Grande river.

One evening, as I walked out of the prayer meeting, alone, feeling quiet, probably not thinking too much, I looked out over that view, and suddenly, some deep chord struck in me. . . I stood stock still for a long time. . . I felt as if I had seen this a thousand times before, and as if it was a deep, deep blessing to be there. . . A quiet, tingling thrill went thru my body — a feeling I treasured for a long time afterwards.

It certainly is a sacred mountain. I had just experienced one of its blessings. . .

the beginning of Lama (at least it's the story I heard)

The story I heard is that Lama was started because of a vision.

Steve Durkee — from the family who has the Durkee spice industry (formerly Scottish pirates, who got into spices as a sideline. . .) — was living the life of a wild young artist in New York City. One day he had a clear vision of a mountainside, with a beautiful view of the desert and a big river. He and his lady Barbara and one other couple headed into the Southwest looking for it. After a long search, they found a mountain called Lama — and it was the place he had seen. . . The mountain is a holy mountain, revered by the Indians. The high altitude, the pure, dry air, the wondrous view — all have their effect. It is a spiritual place.

a spiritual community

And Lama became, first and foremost, a spiritual community. The people there are deeply influenced by Eastern religion and philosophy, especially Sufism, Buddhism, and Hinduism. There are also Christian and Native American influences. Many different masters of many different faiths and disciplines have gone there, and taught there.

Zen and Sufi activities

Special ceremonies include Zen *sesshin* — or intensive periods of meditation — and Sufi group activities, which are always theatrical and fun, especially their dancing and music. Lama became a place of pilgrimage and joy for Sufis, because a very high, beloved Sufi master is buried there, in his own grove high up the mountain — Murshid Samuel Lewis, or Sufi Sam, as he was called.

Sufi dancing is a beautiful form of meditation in action.

Here's one dance:

Everyone stands in a large circle, holding hands. Everyone sings a simple, repetitive, and gently melodic song. The Sufi songs (which are mantras) are often hauntingly beautiful, with minor key melodies, like Gregorian chants. . . The dance steps are simple and beautiful, too: the whole group sweeps into the center, holding hands, moving in together as close as possible, raising hands high into the air, and then moving out backwards as far as you can extend and still hold hands, so that the circle grows from a cluster in the center to its full limits, and then it breaks apart and people move still further out, spinning around, arms in the air. . . then you join hands together again, and repeat, and repeat. . . The dancing is wonderful to watch, and fun to do. And it has a strong, high effect on the dancers, leaving everyone with a feeling of well-being, togetherness, and high energy. . .

The Sufi dance is a beautiful blend of movement, music, and meditation. . .

Sufi dance: movement, music, & meditation

Every Sunday, anyone and everyone is invited to Lama. During the summer, there are often over a hundred people there, many of them coming from nearby Taos — spiritual seekers, hippies, tourists. . . a mixed crowd. Many attend the prayer meetings, which are very open, free gatherings, involving a lot of vocal music, rich harmonies.

Sundays at Lama

My friend Surya Bhakti, from the Floating Lotus, was there at Lama. It was good to reconnect with him once again. I thought of the times we used to spend together, with the Lotus. At those times, I had had a lot of questions for Surya, questions of all kinds. He had been a teacher for me, with his mysterious presence and his rich past. . . Now it was different. I had very few questions. We just enjoyed being together.

Surya — a mysterious presence & a rich past

At that time, Surya was doing a radio show, and he cajoled Carol and me into doing it with him. It was for children, called "The Adventures of Monkey," based on the many stories of Hanuman, the Super-Monkey that keeps appearing thruout the Ramayana, in Hindu literature. We taped it at Lama, using all kinds of weird musical effects, creating storms and battles with demons and supernatural

The Adventures of Monkey

feats and all kinds of things that kids really love. Surya has made a whole series of these tapes — I think they're brilliant.

Surya played with the kids, too, in very beautiful ways. Every afternoon he'd get together with all the kids that lived at Lama, perhaps 15 of them, aged 2-14, and they would dance, and play music together, and tell stories, sitting in a circle, and sing. . .

kids

Everyone took turns spending one morning or afternoon with the kids one day a week. It was a beautiful, successful system — it gave the parents free time, and it gave everybody a chance to relate to the kids in their own individual ways. . . We had a gas together. . .

Every kid is a genius. The nature of childhood and the nature of theater and magic are very close. We explored the woods, played in old abandoned shacks, fed the animals, did gymnastics — and it was constant improvisation, wild imagination, always with a sense of magic. . .

I started hearing and writing poems. . . sometimes very strange —

>Waves crashed on the showery rocks
>   Children danced on the sand
>Wild movement, freedom, bliss
>   Children dance on the sand
>
>From out of the waves, spirits appear!
>   Shining, silvery, spirits of the sea
>Called forth by the children's dancing joy
>   Summoned forth by a child's free energy. . .
>
>The spirits told the children wondrous words
>   Of the magic beings they really are
>Every child is inflamed with magic power
>   Every child is a showering star!
>
>The children see, and hear, and know
>   Strange and wondrous tho it seems
>None of the children will ever forget
>   Seeing their visions and dreaming their dreams

SOME OF THE PEOPLE at Lama — and more and more people all over — are relating deeply to the ancient, beautiful spiritual awareness of the Native Americans. Several people at Lama were involved with the Native American Church. Nearly every night, as the sun went down, I'd hear their chanting, strong, powerful, rhythmic, coming from somewhere on the side of the sacred mountain. On very special occasions, they would take peyote, and chant all night.

Native American spiritual teachings

There are many teachings to be found within this country's own ancient traditions, truly sacred, truly holy, leading to deep understanding.

It is so important that the Native American traditions, like the Tibetan tradition and all other ancient but still surviving traditions, be preserved — continued and understood. It is time for modern Western culture to rediscover its long-forgotten roots.

There is a chant called Navajo Beautyway, a prayer to always take with you. Roughly translated:

an Indian prayer to write down and carry with you

Navajo Beautyway

> I will be happy forever, nothing can hinder me
> I will walk with beauty before me
> I will walk with beauty behind me
> I will walk with beauty above me
> I will walk with beauty below me
> I will walk with beauty around me
> My words will be beautiful
> All my ways are beautiful. . .

I wrote these words down, and carried them with me, in a little bag. . . It worked. . .

up to Sufi Sam's grave, & then to the Eagle's Nest

I took a few days off from the busy schedule and wandered further up the mountain behind Lama, first up to the grave of Sufi Sam and then up further, to a funky retreat shelter, over 10,000 feet up, which was called the "Eagle's Nest"...

At first I wondered what I was doing there... And then I became aware that it was so totally quiet — no traffic, not even any crickets, not even any birds — that all I could hear was the noise inside my own head. It sounded like a radio, droning on and on, words and music, complete with static...

I sat and meditated, trying not to reject my noisy mind, but trying to just let it go... letting it become more quiet...

After some time, the silence and I became one...

Lama was beautiful — a time of much hard work and growth and wonder. But I felt an impulse to continue my pilgrimage in another direction, and I trusted that impulse. My inner voice told me to go back to the Tibetan Center in Berkeley. I knew I had something to learn there... And besides, that strange Tibetan teacher kept popping up in my dreams...

Tibetan Buddhism

I WENT BACK to Berkeley, to Tarthang Tulku Rinpoche's Center — at that time it was just a tiny house on Webster Street. I asked him if there were any opportunities to study and work with him. I ended up staying there for three years and three months. . . And the education I received there was, and continues to be, a strong influence in my life.

The next step in my education

Tarthang Tulku is called 'Rinpoche' (*rim* po shay) by his students. Actually, it's a common name for a high Tibetan lama. Chogyam Trungpa, too, is called Rinpoche. And Dudjom Rinpoche, the head of the Nyingma School of Tibetan Buddhism. And Kalu Rinpoche. And many others. Tarthang said 'Rinpoche' meant teacher. It literally means 'precious jewel', or the one who carries with him the precious jewel of the *Dharma* — the teaching of the Buddha, the real understanding of the nature of the universe. . .

Tarthang Tulku Rinpoche

Tarthang was born in Tibet 40-some years ago, and was recognized before he was 7 years old to be the reincarnation of the previous leader of Tarthang monastery, a large and well-known intellectual and spiritual center in Eastern Tibet. He underwent a rigorous training — a more complete education than any I ever imagined, which culminated in a three year, three month solitary retreat. He emerged as a person of deep understanding and very skillful means to accomplish whatever is necessary.

I was drawn to him because I sensed, even from the very beginning, that here was a man who is a repository of many of the teachings of very ancient traditions, which have been almost completely forgotten by our Western culture, with its left-brain-hemisphere orientation. We've denied the functions of the right hemisphere of the cerebral cortex, and therefore denied our intuition, our deep understanding within, our psychic powers, our magic, our spiritual nature.

repository of ancient traditions

The Tibetan culture, so isolated until 1949 from the ravages of the modern world, has retained several strong and continuous lineages, the oldest of which, the Nyingma,

Unbroken lineage

goes back thousands of years, to the original Shakyamuni Buddha in India, and even beyond.

Tarthang is in some ways very traditional. He wants the lineage to continue in America. Of course, he is adapting constantly to the huge cultural differences between Tibet and America. But he tries to retain all that he can of the original culture.

the puja

Central to his life, and central to the life of his Nyingma Meditation Center, are the ceremonies, or *pujas*. The closest thing in the West to a puja, that I know of, is the Catholic mass. And perhaps some forms of alchemy or 'esoteric' practices. The puja is a powerful, uplifting experience, involving music, chanting mantra, blessing of food, purification, creating a mandala, prayers, visualization, silent meditation, blessing of everyone, and many other elements. . . It

getting back to the roots of the sacred experience, within each one of us

is magic. It is alchemy: it transmutes negative energy into higher energy, more useful energy, awareness, openness, understanding. It is brilliant sacred theater, just as I had been hoping to find, getting back to the roots, within the sacred experience, within the depths of each of us. It has a deep effect on participants, beyond words. . .

Central to the puja is the creation of the *mandala*. The best explanation I have found of the mandala is, interestingly enough, in a book called *Seven Arrows*, written by a Native American teacher named Hyemeyohsts Storm. Rinpoche often said that there was a deep connection and similarity between the teachings, and even the races, of the Tibetans and the American Indians — which supports the theory of the wanderings of ancient tribes from Mongolia (right next to Tibet) over the Bering Strait and into North America. I gave Rinpoche a copy of *Seven Arrows*, in fact: he looked through it slowly, with deep interest. He kept pointing to the pictures of the American Indians and saying, "They look just like Tibetans. . . They are the same race. . ."

the mandala, the medicine wheel

Seven Arrows deals with the medicine wheel — which is the same thing as a mandala. The medicine wheel, the mandala, can be created from anything — a circle of rocks on the ground, a painted shield, a circle marking off a dance area (like the cornmeal mandala of the Floating Lotus), a painting, a button, an elaborate construction of wood and cloth with statues of deities sitting within, as in the puja, or the inside of a sweat lodge — all are mandalas, or medicine wheels... You are a medicine wheel. We are all a medicine wheel, a mandala. The earth is a mandala, and the solar system, and the galaxy, and your eye ... circles within circles, each reflecting the other.

A medicine wheel is anything you choose to symbolically represent the entire universe. And it actually has the power to reflect the whole, because any piece of the universe reflects the whole of the universe... It is all the same substance, the same form, repeated endlessly... Within the atom, the galaxy is mirrored...

The Indians say that the entire universe is within the sweat lodge — and it is true. Deep understanding of whole systems, visions, can be found in the darkness of the sweat lodge — and the darkness of your own room.

The puja creates a mandala of the altar, and of the entire room. All the participants become part of the mandala. A stage, an audience, a dance, a movie screen, a record, even a TV screen — these are all mandalas, on some deep level... There is power in a mandala, power we are just now discovering, power to heal, to uplift, to give visions, to give deep understanding and meaning to life...

There are infinite possibilities...

We had classes, too, at the Tibetan Center — classes of an amazing variety, scope, and effectiveness. Often they would consist of group yoga, like breathing in unison together, or chanting together, or physical exercises, often requiring (and thereby creating) great physical strength. I slowly began to realize that what we were learning was a blend of many, many different categories of Western thinking, simultaneously evolving into a rich, holistic discovery... We were doing 'spiritual' practices, we were learning 'philosophy', and 'psychology', employing 'Gestalt' and 'bio-energetics' and 'polarity therapy' and 'Alexander' techniques (and even some 'primal therapy' techniques), 'psychodrama', music, athletics, dream work, intellectual research, even physics, astrology, theater, and physical work... So many things which we are used to thinking of in terms of different and somehow unrelated categories were treated simultaneously, within a system that has a wonderful understanding of the human being as

a wheel inside a wheel

a microcosm which reflects the macrocosm

there is power in a mandala

classes

a holistic system of study

a deep teaching: ultimate truth, relative truths

an organic whole within the mandala of the universe.

There is an ultimate truth behind, and within, the myriad of relative truths. Within that ultimate, there are no distinctions, no categories, no differences between one thing and another, no 'things' at all, in fact. Ultimately, physics and psychology and philosophy and biology, etc, etc, all lead to the same truth: the nature of existence. But each must transcend its own (relative) form to reach it. . . We are a part of the universe, we are flowers, we are stars. Ultimately, there is no difference, it's all the same, it's all a form of energy, and it's really totally devoid of form (*shunya*). This is the deepest discovery and teaching of Buddha. . .

I was encountering a tradition which actually understood and taught these things. . . and the classes and the personal instruction were intense, shimmering, and deeply inspired. . .

There were times when Tarthang's words would burst forth like exquisite poetry. . . He never bothered to learn English very well (at least when I knew him), and so he used it spontaneously, creatively, with a beautiful, wild imagination. . .

words from a class

In his classes he spoke words like these (I copied these words during one of his talks. . . He talked faster than I could write, so I could just grab pieces of what he said here and there, and the result is pure poetry. . .):

> Every day, a new world.
>   Every day, a new life.
> Be happy, and in harmony
>   Without discrimination, without problems
> Free. . .
>   No walls, discrimination, pollution, noise, high, low,
>   color, shape. . . But all purity. . .
> The ultimate can be brought into the Now, the daily life.
> Free, very free
>   All bondage burned away,
>   No attachment
> The spiritual person
>   is free like a bird. . .
> Happy is not happy to him,
>   Sadness is not sadness to him
> Pain is not pain to him
>   Pleasure is not pleasure to him. . .
>
>   . . . The world is a one-night's dream
>   and now we are dreaming. . .

I learned so much about a man named Padma Sambhava while at the Tibetan Center. He is like the Jesus of Tibet, and many people feel very devotional towards him. . . His name means "Lotus Born," because according to legend he was born out of a huge lotus flower. The histories are full of many, many miraculous tales of his life. He was a truly great magician and master — that is, he *is*, because one of the minor powers he has is immortality. And he can change his shape at will. He is alive and well today in many, many forms.

Padma Sambhava, the 'Lotus Born', the Jesus of Tibet

The only time I ever heard Tarthang Tulku mention his own personal achievement in this country was when he said, "I have introduced many, many Americans to Padma Sambhava." This is indeed one of Tarthang's finest contributions to the West, among many others. . .

Padma Sambhava is the father of Buddhist 'Tantra'. . . Just as the *sutras* (84,000 of them) are the oral teachings which the Buddha gave, the *tantras* are the written teachings of Padma Sambhava. The sutras of Buddha are brilliantly intelligent — obviously the conceptualizations of a genius mind, masterpieces of inspired thinking and clear reasoning: a supremely skillful use of rational mind which goes beyond rational mind. . . Buddha obviously spoke to a culture which was highly civilized, very refined. . .

the father of Buddhist Tantra

The tantras of Padma Sambhava, on the other hand, are pragmatic and practical. They are things you do — practices — rather than things you hear intellectually. . . They are designed for a culture whose thinkers are more skeptical, more belligerent, more pragmatic. . . America today, the western world today, is ready for both the sutras and the tantras. And they are being translated and absorbed, in many, many forms. . .

Padma Sambhava mastered Buddhism at a very young age. They say he was the student of Ananda, Buddha's most beloved disciple. But he spent many, many more years wandering, searching out teachers, meditating in graveyards, giving his life totally, gathering teachings from many different sources. . . These teachings took form as the *tantras*.

The tantras, at least until now, have been grossly misunderstood and sadly misinterpreted in the West. Most people think they are only "The Yoga of Sex," and no more. But

the power of the tantras

they are much more. They are a vast variety of practices and meta-practices, embracing every path, and every level of being, rejecting nothing. The tantras made Padma Sambhava capable of bringing Buddhism to cultures very different from India, such as Tibet. He adapted Buddhism brilliantly, presenting many totally new techniques to the Tibetans, which were specially tailored for them, easy for them to grasp, and make their own. This was the power and effectiveness of the tantras.

I saw that Tarthang Tulku, too (and Chogyam Trungpa, and many others), is very much like Padma Sambhava, in that he is constantly searching for new techniques to bring his understanding into a foreign culture, one so very different from his homeland. And I realized that by living with this man, and by learning about Padma Sambhava, my own path had come into a much clearer focus. Like Padma Sambhava, like Tarthang Tulku, I began to feel that my presence on this planet was chosen in order to first understand and then to communicate the teachings of one culture to another. . . In connecting with the Tibetan traditions I had discovered one of the sanest cultures on our planet, a culture and a philosophy which has a lot to teach us. And I, too, became committed above all to finding effective techniques for us Westerners. . . techniques for problem-solving, for personal growth, for realization.

problem-solving, personal growth, realization

Carol is with Chogyam Trungpa, Rinpoche

Carol has been with Chogyam Trungpa, Rinpoche, in Boulder, Colorado for several years now. He, too, is a strong Tibetan teacher. But his approach is more radical, much less traditional, at least to outward appearances. He's written many fine books, including *Meditation in Action*, *Born in Tibet*, and *Cutting Through Spiritual Materialism*. He speaks brilliantly.

I've visited his center in Boulder a few times. And I've been very impressed with what they're building, and the strength of the people there. I watch Trungpa Rinpoche with deep interest — he is a wild innovator, and a free spirit.

Sometimes, things would get very rough at the Tibetan Center. The work was very difficult and demanding. Living there was not easy. At times, I would dream of just leaving, giving it all up, and going up to Oregon, and finding me a funky country band to play music in. Who knows? Maybe I'll do it someday. . . There are infinite possibilities. . .

After the Nyingma Meditation Center had been established for three years, attempting a fairly traditional type of training for full-time, fully committed students, Rinpoche started an entirely new kind of educational program, the Nyingma Institute. The title was originally the Nyingma Psychology Institute, but the American Psychology Association objected to his use of the word 'psychology' — although that's exactly what it is: the 'study of mind' (not 'the study of behavior', as it is still all too often defined in the West. . .).

Nyingma Institute: Eastern teachings in Western form

The Nyingma Institute presents Eastern and Eastern-related teachings in a Western form. It offers classes to the general public, unlike the original center. A program many of us were following was called 'Studies of Consciousness' — it was originally called psychology. Classes have been very effective. Tarthang Tulku has found a very good form in which to teach.

Studies of Consciousness

The immediate success of the Nyingma Institute was spectacular — over 400 people enrolled the first quarter. There have also been intensive summer programs for professionals in the psychological and medical and scientific fields, which have had a beautiful impact.

Trungpa is doing a similar, but even much larger, summer program in Boulder called the Naropa Institute. Allen Ginsberg, Herbert Guenther, Robert Bly, Ram Dass, and many others are teaching there. Someone described it as a 'spiritual Woodstock'. . .

Naropa Institute

At Nyingma Institute, I specialized somewhat in 'Kum Nye' — it means literally 'working with the body' or even 'body massage'. It is an endless series of Tibetan techniques which developed from the tantras. Usually, they are physical, although there is great variation. Kum Nye has had a great deal of impact on professional therapists of many types, because it involves a wealth of techniques which recent Western psychological and physiological studies are now exploring. The exercises are amazingly similar (sometimes exactly identical) to Gestalt exercises, polarity, Alexander technique, bio-energetics, pressure-point massage, hatha yoga, and a wealth of other techniques, East and West.

'Kum Nye': physical exercises

The physical exercises are effective. They leave you feeling very light physically, and healthy, even glowing. . . People's eyes were always exceptionally bright and clear after classes.

psycho-drama at the Tibetan Center

exploring family strife & death

ONE MORNING, 15 or 20 of the 'older students' went downstairs together into the dark, carpeted basement yoga room of the Meditation Center. Rinpoche joined us and said, "OK, now let's do some drama". . . And he set up an improvised psychodrama, in which we played family members, who get into a violent argument at the dinner table, during which the father has a heart attack, is rushed to the hospital, and dies. I played one of the sons. It was an unforgettable experience. We found ourselves immediately embroiled in the middle of a very emotional situation that all of us could relate to individually: family strife. It was brilliant improvisation, because no one was concerned at all about technique, or about how they looked, or acted — it was spontaneous, here-and-now gut level emotional theater. And it had a strong effect on all involved. We learned much about death, and strong emotions, and each other, and ourselves.

Then we did a second little play, in which the mother died, alternating roles so that everyone got to play a major role in the family.

Then we all sat around the girl who had played the mother. She had died, and she had a sheet over her. Rinpoche said, "Imagine that this is your mother, and that she has just died. . . How do you feel?"

This was a powerful method of teaching. I began to deeply appreciate my mother in a new way. Suddenly, there was a desire in me to express my love for her — something I saw I had never really done. I felt exhausted after that class — and strangely exhilarated at the same time.

meditation and great art create receptivity

We were being shown many, many different forms of meditation at the Tibetan Center. Meditation and great art have much in common. They put us into a receptive state. . . and then they give us their teachings, which we really discover within ourselves.

I worked at Dharma Press, the Tibetan Center's press, for two years. It was a difficult but beautiful experience: doing books gets into your blood, the same way theater does. Besides commercial work, we printed and typeset things for the Center, such as *Calm and Clear, Legend of the Great Stupa, Crystal Mirror, Gesar, Sacred Art of Tibet*, and a lot of other posters and art work. . . Many of Tarthang's students were at work translating ancient and modern Tibetan works, which were in danger of being lost totally. . .

Time passes, and all things change. . .

I started feeling some cultural/ideological/spiritual/vibrational differences with the teachings and the lifestyle at the Tibetan Center. . . My experience with the book *Calm and Clear* is a good example. I typeset that book while at Dharma Press. It is a traditional Tibetan work, written by one of the greatest of Nyingma teachers several hundred years ago.

There is a meditation given in the book, which I tried many times to get into; it is designed to try to discourage people from physical relationships. It involves imagining the person you desire the most — your ideal lover. . . In your mind's eye, you look at them, imagine them, and see what feelings arise in you. Then you imagine removing their layer of skin, and looking at the blood and muscle and all the inner workings — observing what feelings arise. Roam thru their body, and meditate upon the fact that every body is nothing other than a collection of blood, bone, mucus, puss, excrement, piss, etc, etc. . .

I tried, several times, to do the meditation as instructed — even though my inner voice was telling me that it wasn't exactly my trip. . . Yet each time I did it, as I got into the blood and puss and excrement part, a very clear voice would come along and say, "Yeah, but look at how *beautifully* all that shit is put together!" And the whole meditation would totally fall apart — sometimes even transforming into an experience of deep wonder and love for all people. . . I couldn't help but marvel at the beauty of it all. . . Our bodies are truly exquisite creations of a divine love. . .

I finally told Rinpoche of my lack of success in this form of meditation. He laughed, in a beautifully open way, and said, "Yab-yum for you!" It was a remark I really cherished:

Dharma Press: 'printer's ink gets into your blood'

Calm & Clear

a meditation upon our bodies —

blood, bone, mucus, puss, excrement, etc. . .

. . .beautifully put together

'Yab-yum'   "yab-yum" is the Tibetan equivalent of "yin and yang" or even "Shiva-Shakti": ie, male-female... It was his way of saying that he recognized that my path was not one of renunciation...

American Tantra

a small thing happens on Telegraph Ave.

THEN ONE SUNNY DAY late in the mild winter, while strolling down Telegraph Avenue in Berkeley, a very small thing happened...

Many people dislike Telegraph Ave — and for a lot of good reasons: it's dirty, it's crowded, it's somewhat crazy, the energy is very intense, and there's raggedy, funky street people and other assorted weirdos on it, selling dope and asking for spare change... But I love it — it's a streetscene that has created so much creative juice that the entire country, the entire world, has felt it. It's a phenomenal energy center, always changing, always giving birth to something ... and it's sometimes a painful birth...

Anyway...

I was strolling down Telegraph and saw a lovely lady handing out some kind of leaflet — which is nothing unusual, except for her smile and her quiet vibrations and exceptional beauty, in both inner and outer ways... I noticed as I approached her that she handed it out to very few people, only those that she seemed to have a moment of some kind of special contact with. I drew near ... we looked at each other (she *was* beautiful...), she smiled openly and handed me a small piece of paper. I smiled, and walked on by, and started reading it, quite skeptically. There's a huge amount of weird literature of all descriptions being handed out on Telegraph Ave.

a lady with an inner and an outer beauty

a smile

and a leaflet

But I was in for a surprise: the words I read struck me deeply... It seemed years ahead of what I had been dreaming of: it was a brilliant adaptation of the teachings I had been studying to the American mentality and awareness and lifestyle.

The leaflet started with the words —

>   TWELVE PATHWAYS
>   to the higher consciousness planes
>   of unconditional love and oneness
>
> Liberating my conscious-awareness
> 1. I am freeing myself from security, sensation, and power addictions that make me try to forcefully control situations in my life, and thus destroy my serenity and keep me from loving myself and others...

'Pathways to the higher consciousness planes of... love and oneness'

and it ended with the words —

> Realizing cosmic consciousness....
> 12. I am perceiving everyone, including myself, as an awakening being who is here to claim his or her birthright of the higher consciousness planes of unconditional love and oneness.

The leaflet was from a place called "The Living Love Center"... That name was difficult for me to accept — it seemed a little blatant... But the words of the leaflet struck a deep chord within me... I felt they said in a simple, easily graspable way many of the things I had very slowly been growing to understand during the course of my search.

a deep chord within me

My study at the Tibetan Center had proved fruitful in many ways... and yet I was becoming discontented with it... I had learned so many useful and beautiful things, things I wanted to share with others. Yet most people don't have ears to hear them within the forms of a foreign tradition.

I began to see an amazing parallel between the time when Buddhism was introduced into Tibet and our time now, when Buddhism and many, many other teachings are being introduced and absorbed into the West...

an interesting parallel

(Some of the following is repetitious — in many ways I just said similar things. But repetition can be useful... Just relax and enjoy this... or flip to something else...)

Buddha — the historical Shakyamuni Buddha — taught in India, about five centuries before Christ... His teachings are the heart of all true Buddhism — whether it's Zen (from Japan) or C'han (from China) or Theravadin (from Ceylon and Southeast Asia) or Tantric (from Tibet)... Buddha obviously taught a very sophisticated, highly intellectual,

history repeats itself

brilliantly educated group of people. His recorded talks (or 'sutras') are the work of a brilliant mind — both vast and analytical — a master of psychology and philosophy. . .

Over a thousand years after Buddha's lifetime, his teachings had spread widely — to China, Japan, and Southeast Asia — but they hadn't penetrated into Tibet because, as the Tibetans freely admit today, they were far too wild and hostile and aggressive to relate to anything on such subtle psychological and philosophical planes. . . In fact, the Tibetans describe themselves as being 'blue-faced monkeys' before Buddhism came — fierce fighters who would paint their faces blue when fighting . . . with fierce magician-priests of an ancient religion called *Bon*. . .

Padma Sambhava & the tantras

Then, in about 800 AD (according to Western reckoning), a man named Padma Sambhava came along. . . He was born in an ancient land called Urgyan or Uddiyana — probably part of Nepal today — and he spent many years in India, mastering the teachings of Buddha. . . And it is said that, in many ways, he even went beyond the teachings of Buddha, because he managed to adapt them to a form that the wild Tibetan people could deeply relate to. . . The sutras of the Buddha inspired the 'tantras' of Padma Sambhava — in his hands, the teachings of Buddha were translated into very powerful, physical practices and teachings which the Tibetans could readily understand. . .

a foreign tradition becomes a living, transformative tool. . .

Just as Hui Neng had done in China — the brilliant, illiterate Sixth Patriarch who brought Buddhism to the common people — Padma Sambhava molded a foreign tradition into a living, transformative tool for the people. The whole Tibetan culture absorbed the teachings of Buddha, and the culture transformed. No longer 'blue-faced monkeys', they are, in my opinion, one of the sanest cultures that has survived into the 20th century, with many deep teachings on many levels for many different types of people. . .

History is repeating itself. The Tibetans (and so many others) are bringing Buddhism, and Hinduism, and other teachings, into the West. And they encounter a culture which is much wilder and more aggressive than they can even comprehend: *America*.

I applaud the efforts of teachers from the East in America today. I know it is difficult for them. . . India and Tibet are so much more civilized and sensitive than we are, in so many ways. The closest thing to the East on our continent is the American Indian culture, which I pray is being re-born again (and after reading *Seven Arrows*, and hearing of Richard Kastl and Rolling Thunder, I *know* it is being reborn again). . .

The East comes to the West

There were times when Tarthang Rinpoche, a Tibetan in Berkeley, used to lament that our philosophy is so weak, and our language is so limited, that it is very difficult to translate what he knows into terms we can understand. . . And there were so many things that Tarthang could not accept about the American culture — so many things that, unfortunately, led many of his students to end up rejecting their backgrounds, rejecting others, and rejecting themselves. . .

Yet, Tarthang is trying so hard to accept it. . . and he is always changing, and growing, and trying new things. And he is a brilliant teacher, always focused on finding *skillful means* to accomplish what he most desires — easing the burdens of all humankind, bringing light and happiness and peace to all. . .

My meditation, too, had become trying to find *skillful means* — ways to absorb the teachings, and to communicate the teachings. . . bringing light and happiness and peace to all. . .

When I read that leaflet on Telegraph Avenue, I had the feeling that here was someone who had clearly expressed what I had begun to dream of expressing: the deep, ancient teachings clearly translated into words that have meaning for the people of this country. . . It is tantra for Americans.

tantra for Americans

I went to a Sunday night open house at the Living Love Center. . .

an open house at the Living Love Center

I had been transcribing a talk of Tarthang's for most of the day. It was a particularly positive talk, in which he was saying things such as (roughly paraphrased), "We can create a paradise here and now. . . because, what is paradise? It is a level of consciousness, which we can attain — a state where all negative emotions become changed, transmuted, into perfect balance." A young, relaxed student at the Living Love Center named Randy stood up and began to casually rap. "You know," he said, "we can really create a paradise, here and now. . ." His ideas almost exactly paralleled Tarthang's — many of his words were even identical.

Then Ken Keyes, the founder, spoke. It was beautifully impressive to me: the subject and even the form of his talk was, one one level, pure Buddhism — yet it was not presented as a religion or philosophy of any kind, and it was devoid of Eastern terms or foreign concepts: it was brilliantly translated into the language and consciousness of this culture.

His talk outlined the 'four universal truths' of Buddha, the first talk the Buddha ever gave. Ken quite simply and clearly established the obvious truths that (1) there are a great many problems in the world today — wars, famines, failing economic and ecological systems, etc — and almost everybody has personal problems, too, based on the desire for security, sensation, and/or power; and (2) there is a single, basic cause for all of these problems, whether on a global or personal level: we have problems because we are *addicted* to something — to security, sensation, and/or power. This addiction is defined very clearly as an emotion-backed demand; (3) once this cause is seen, we discover that there is an end to all our problems — there is no need for us to suffer, or to be frustrated, etc, at all; and (4) there are many techniques available to us to achieve this state of consciousness which overcomes all problems, which frees a person to do exactly what he or she wants to do, which leads to deep understanding, even 'cosmic consciousness'. . .

His talk was simple and clear — and effective. People were obviously ready for it, and moved by it. The audience reacted strongly, and positively. . .

Ken Keyes is now in his late 50s. He was trained in psychology, and then went into business (real estate — which has proved useful). When he was 26 years old, he was struck with polio, which totally incapacitated both his arms and his legs — he has a bit of control of one arm. He went thru a lot of changes, a lot of pain. He married twice, and divorced twice. . . In the early 70s, he met a young kid in Miami who totally blew his mind. The kid was a student of Chogyam Trungpa's, and he spent several weeks with Ken, telling him of Buddhism and its possibilities for the

'We can create a paradise, here & now.'

universal truths

which lead to deep understanding, even 'cosmic consciousness'

Ken Keyes

and a young kid

West. Ken became a student of Trungpa's, and later got into Baba Ram Dass. And then, he had some brilliant breakthrus, which he is able to clearly communicate to others. *The Handbook to Higher Consciousness* and the Living Love Center (now the Cornucopia Institute in Kentucky) are the results of his growth and his work. . .

The Handbook to Higher Consciousness

I talked to Ken afterwards. He was delighted to hear that I was a student at the Tibetan Center and the Nyingma Institute, and he told me what I had felt all along: it was all based on his understanding of Buddhist principles.

You may think that my interest in it because it is *Buddhist* is purist or narrow-minded. The 'Buddhism' of the Living Love Center impressed me because, over the years, I had come to deeply admire the effectiveness and directness of the Buddha's teachings. It combines a brilliant, progressive philosophy with a very simple, easy to grasp psychology. It is very scientific: everything is examined personally, skeptically; nothing is accepted on pure faith alone. Buddhism can adapt very effectively to the West. . .

the teachings are scientific

Einstein once said: "The religion of the future will be a cosmic religion. It should transcend a personal God and avoid dogmas and theology. Covering both the natural and spiritual, it should be based on a religious sense arising from the experience of all things, natural and spiritual, and a meaningful unity. Buddhism answers this description. . . If there is any religion that would cope with modern scientific needs it would be Buddhism."

Einstein on religion

Yet, I'm not rejecting any other paths — there are many, many ways to climb the mountain. And there are many other traditions and teachings which are being absorbed into the West.

The Living Love Center blew my mind and opened my heart.

It offered, at that time, a 'consciousness growth seminar' and a 'consciousness growth intensive' each month — each a week-end long experience. The 'seminar' was relatively low key, an introduction to, and an application of, the *Handbook to Higher Consciousness*. It had been especially successful in relating to older people. The techniques are very useful for dissolving problems, making relationships work, living a useful and happy and fully-appreciated life. This is

The Living Love Center blew my mind and opened my heart

131

techniques which work continually, on a gut level

what I'd been searching for — it's what my study of Buddhism had come to mean: something which could be passed on to large numbers of people, which could make their lives more complete and happier... The 'intensive' had been especially successful in relating to younger people. It accomplished in one weekend what I had been searching for for years: it took the ideas of the *Handbook*, of Buddhism, of so many consciousness growth systems of all kinds, and gave me techniques to use these ideas continually, on a gut level...

the weekend 'intensive'

I took the weekend 'intensive'... Forty people were together in one big room, with very few breaks, from Friday evening to Sunday evening. We began the weekend as strangers; we ended it as heart-friends.

Friday night, about 50 of us strangers sat around the walls of a large, deeply carpeted room. We were asked to turn in a list of questions that had been sent to us — a kind of simple but thought-provoking take-home test which required that you had read *The Handbook to Higher Consciousness*. Most of the questions related directly to the book, but there were other questions — deep, personal ones — What do you think is your deepest problem? What are the things about you that you really don't want others to know?

questions: what is your deepest problem?

what is the best thing about you?

The tests were collected, put aside, and completely ignored.

Then Randy started rapping. He asked everyone to tell what they thought was the best thing about themselves. Someone said, 'My intelligence'... I said, 'Sometimes I can really help people'... Someone else said, 'Being tall'... Randy said, 'The deep calm within'...

Then, everyone got up and listened to each other's hearts... just casually walking around, placing your head on someone's heart, listening, going on to another person... It became a strangely wonderful way to meet these people...

It all started out on a very positive, strong note. Then we did our first 'circle', and things started to get intense... We divided into small groups of four people each, and sat in a circle together. The first circle began with this question: What was the situation in the last 48 hours or so that got you the most uptight? Each person related the incident fully.

Then the staff went to work on them, with questions. What was the *real* problem in that situation?. . . The problem is fully explored, and it always leads to an *addiction*: an emotion-backed demand. The basic supposition of the whole system is that *every* problem is just a reflection of an addiction. . .

Then the specific addiction is pinpointed as fully as possible, and stated as simply as possible. (It's amazing how elusive the rational mind and ego are, making this step difficult. . .) Once the basic addiction is discovered, the innovative step takes place: the step called 'reprogramming'. Many people, including me at first, balk at that terminology. Ken has been influenced by John Lilly, who did the famous sensory deprivation experiments while suspended in water, in total isolation. . . he also worked with dolphins. One of Lilly's books is called *Programming and Metaprogramming in the Human Biocomputer*. I was skeptical of this reprogramming technique at first. But I am a researcher, and I tried to get into it as fully as possible. And I found it works. The theory is that you can balance, control, and even transmute previously overwhelming 'negative' or 'separating' emotions by deeply imbedding into your biocomputer (or mind. . .) short, simple phrases which you know intellectually to be true. Thru reprogramming, you can actually change your previously 'uncontrollable' emotional responses to things.

The addiction is pinpointed, as simply and specifically as possible (such as, 'I am addicted to women' or 'I need people's respect' or 'I need my parents' approval' or whatever it is that's causing the problem. *Note*: the thing you're addicted to is not *bad*, or negative in any way. There is nothing wrong at all with desiring women or respect or approval, for example — it's the uptightness, the emotional constriction that goes along with it that is unnecessary and can be let go of). Then the person finds two or three short, direct reprogramming phrases (such as, 'I am enough' or 'I don't need her love', or 'I don't *need* their respect'). Once they've been selected, the actual reprogramming takes place. The person gets back into the painful situation he or she has just related, eyes closed. We found it very easy to recall those emotions. Adrenalin flows easily — the heavier the situation was, the better. Then the person repeats the

our first 'circle'

'reprogramming'

the heavier the situation, the better

133

effective techniques

phrases with as much intensity as they can muster (usually into a pillow if they're shouting. It isn't necessary to be loud, just intense — you can even reprogram silently). . .

The person usually finishes with this phrase:

> The purpose of my life
> is to be free of all addictive traps
> and thus become one with the ocean of living love.

The circles are effective techniques. There were four of them during the weekend — three others dealing with security, sensation (sex), and power addictions.

physical exercises and group explorations

They were interspersed with a wide variety of physical practices and group explorations and sharing. . .

Saturday and Sunday morning began with an intense series of physical exercises, a very powerful form of meditation, which increased the effectiveness of the reprogramming and of the weekend in experience in general. They called it 'chaotic meditation'. It was developed in India by a spiritual leader named Bhagwhan Rajnesh, who has thousands of Western students. He says that this form of meditation is especially adapted for Americans and Western Europeans, who have developed huge, complex rational minds and egos — their strength, and their difficulty. Powerful techniques are required to break thru these barriers to meditation, and to a peaceful, sane life — and he has found some.

'Chaotic meditation' — Rajnesh

It's a very physical form of meditation. Everyone was given a blindfold. Then, with wild, rhythmic, loud music going, and with the staff members banging on drums and tambourines, everyone began jumping as high and as hard as they could, pumping their arms. After 30 seconds, I was exhausted, but I couldn't quit. . . After two minutes, I felt as if I couldn't possibly go on jumping any longer. . . sideaches. . . pain. . . my body was screaming for a rest, and yet the staff members were screaming, "Keep it up! Exhaust yourself!. . . Go beyond your body! Go beyond!" And then, just beyond the point where I felt I was going to collapse, an amazing thing happened: a powerful inner energy took over, and I leapt right beyond my body's narrow limitations. . . I continued jumping, fully, strongly, for 10 minutes, and when we stopped, I could have continued much longer. . . Then we did 10 minutes of total freeform

beyond your body's narrow limitations

expression, whatever we wanted to do, still blind-folded. We had so much energy after all the jumping — people were screaming, being born, dying, flipping out, dancing, everything — that's the chaotic part of the chaotic meditation. Then, everybody started jumping again, vigorously, this time with arms raised high, shouting "Hu. . . hu!. . .hu!" very strongly, from a low gut-level, for 10 more minutes. Again, just when I thought I was going to drop from exhaustion, I connected with that incredible energy! Then, someone shouted "Freeze!" — and we had to stand, arms raised in the air, totally motionless, for another 10 minutes (a technique that Gurdjieff used). Again, after about two minutes, my arms felt totally exhausted. . . but then I was able to simply step outside of my body, into a very quiet, peaceful place, where there was no effort, no pain. It is a very effective form of meditation. Like all meditation, it's difficult to describe in words.

from chaos

. . . into a quiet, peaceful place

It became clear to me that chaotic meditation was doing on a physical gut-level exactly what reprogramming and the rest was doing on an emotional gut-level: finding the energy and light deep within yourself which is powerful enough to dissolve all pain, all imaginary limitations.

finding energy & light deep within

I started getting incredibly enthusiastic, light and high, in spite of myself, during the Intensive. We were actually employing the techniques I had been looking for!

By Sunday night, the group had transformed. Healing miracles had occurred. People looked years younger, and incredibly radiant, and beautiful. I felt totally stoned, loaded on love. . .

I went up to a lovely girl named Becky, who lived at the Center and had worked with us during the Intensive. I told her I felt like running down the street shouting *eureka*. . . she grabbed my hand, and we were out the door, running thru the midnight streets' cool mist, jumping, skipping, shouting

Eureka!

"Eureka!"

It was as if a great weight had been lifted off my shoulders, and head, and heart. . . a weight which I wasn't even fully aware of until I let it go. . .

perfectly compatible with anything

This was for me a very beautiful thing about the Living Love Center, at that time: they didn't present any kind of specific trip at all that you had to accept or align yourself with; it was perfectly compatible with any other system of consciousness growth, or religion, or yogic practice, or philosophy, or whatever... It was a broad system which offered many different kinds of tools for consciousness growth, and the individual could choose which ones fit his or her needs exactly. It accepted everyone, and every activity they were doing. This is why I even called it 'tantra', because I see tantric methods as being those which accept and utilize all forms of energy, all kinds of different activities...

American tantra

Tantra accepts everything — it rejects nothing. Everything is valuable and useful... every moment is grist for the mill.

many changes

Many changes in my life took place in the weeks following the Intensive. I had found effective tools that worked for me: I was free to go anywhere, and to do anything...

It led to my leaving the Tibetan Center — but still retaining a heart-felt connection with Rinpoche... it led to going back to Minnesota to write a paper which turned out to be the seed of this book... It led to becoming aware that there are infinite possibilities!

a new kind of freedom

I felt a new kind of freedom — I realized that there was nothing I really had to do... so I was free to do *anything* — whatever my heart desired... Free to wander, free to dream, free to live my life in any way I wish, and to build whatever I can dream of building...

I started writing, at this time... and writing and playing music — doing whatever my heart told me to do...

I left the Tibetan Center in the Spring. . .

I had gone to the Tibetan Center in a very open way, searching for something — I knew not what. I left with some clear goals and some very useful tools for achieving them. I'll always be thankful to Rinpoche for his energy and guidance and vision.

One of the best teachings I can pass on simply involves "the five wisdoms". . . In Tibetan tradition they teach that there is not just one type of "wisdom," and not just one focus for education and growth, but there are five. Personal growth involves the development of *all* of these areas of understanding. They are

The 'five wisdoms': different areas of growth

—The wisdom that sees the Oneness, the sameness of everything. This involves the ability to enjoy what is given you.

—The "discriminating wisdom," which sees the differences between things. This involves the ability to criticize, and make change.

—The "mirror-like wisdom" which reflects the people and Universe around you. This involves the ability to deeply relate to others.

—The "all-accomplishing wisdom," which can take care of business effortlessly. This involves the ability to manifest what you want on a physical plane.

—The ultimate wisdom, which is the mystical experience. . . the experience of the "Dharmakaya" — or whatever you wish to call it. . . the union with the Universe. . . This involves connecting with your infinite nature. . .

Each individual has their own combination of strengths and weaknesses — each one of us understands some of these wisdoms very well, and is weak in others. The ideal is to master all five of them.

the ideal is to master all five

I spent the Spring and Summer wandering, absorbing. . . First I went to some festivals, in Davis and Sonoma, and then I went back to Minnesota and stayed with my folks for a few months — and got to know them again, and to love them again. . .

Miracles

Kathryn Kuhlman, healer, miracle-worker

ONE NIGHT OF THAT SPRING is unforgettable... My friend Paul Clemens — a close brother from the Tibetan Center and Dharma Press — told me about a woman named Kathryn Kuhlman. She was a very well-known faith healer. She traveled widely, even had her own TV show, and had written a book called *I Believe in Miracles*.

Paul said that his folks had gone to see this woman in Illinois. Paul's father had had bursitis in his left shoulder for 10 years, and he couldn't even lift his arm above his head. He 'just happened' to sit on an aisle seat. As she entered, Kathryn Kuhlman came up that aisle, and as she passed by him, she simply and quickly touched his shoulder. He said it felt like an electric shock thru his entire body and, like a reflex action, his crippled arm shot out in the air. He stretched his arm high over his head for the first time in 10 years, and found to his utter amazement that he was totally cured...

She was coming to Oakland that evening. We decided to see her...

Imagine this:

The steps and sidewalks surrounding the Oakland Auditorium were packed by 3:00 in the afternoon — doors were to open at 6:00; Kathryn Kuhlman was starting a service at 6:30...

People started singing hymns, which would grow and spread thru the crowd... it was a mixed crowd, young, old, black, white, brown, yellow, straight, hip... food was shared... total strangers greeted each other like heart-friends...

The side doors leading to the main floor were reserved for people in wheelchairs and hospital beds, and nurses and attendants... hundreds of sick people, praying to be healed, were being wheeled in, helped in...

The crowd was soon several times larger than the Auditorium could seat — I hadn't been in a dense crowd like that for years, since Altamont... When they finally opened the doors, people were packed together, and most of the crowd had to be turned away. (She was in the Oakland Coliseum the next time, which is much larger. . .) We were some of the very last to get in.

The floor of the Auditorium, the basketball court, was like a huge, open hospital — there were hundreds of wheelchairs, and some beds. . . Energy was so high, positive. . . It was incredible before it even started. . .

There was a large stage at the far end with a grand piano down left, an organ down right, and a choir of about 700 voices filling the upstage area. . . The piano and organ were being played together, beautifully (good sound system), as people entered. . .

Then Kathryn Kuhlman entered, up a side aisle. She is so magnetic that I spotted her immediately and knew it was her, even though I'd never seen her before. She was very tall and slim and graceful. I thought she was somewhere in her early 40s — later I was told that she was 73 years old. She was dressed in a long, simple white dress, with very full, flaring sleeves. She was a white witch. . .

a white witch

The choir sang hymns. . . then she introduced a vocalist, then a very inspired, soaring pianist. There was a beautiful energy behind the music. . . Then, the music quieted, and she started to speak. The lights dimmed. . . She asked everyone to be very still and quiet. The air was charged. After the wave of music, the stillness was very deep. . .

She started by quietly saying something like, "I hope you can understand that *I* am not saying these words. If you don't understand, just shut up and be quiet, for now. . . sit very still, for a moment. . ."

'I hope you can understand that I am not saying these words'

Slowly, with great skill, she created a relaxed, meditative mood. . . She started talking, randomly, spontaneously, about the state of the world, how things look dark in some ways. . . Then she started talking about the healings of Jesus — how he could heal with pure spirit, pure energy, spontaneously. . . She said if we believe healing miracles happened in the past, they can and do happen in the present, because that same healing energy is never born and never dies — it always exists. . . Everything was very still and quiet. . .

139

'Miracles — just like in Jesus's time'

She said she felt the Holy Spirit filling the room, and that when that happened, miracles happen, "just like in Jesus's time — this time is no different. . ."

Suddenly, her right arm shot out, straight and intense, reaching upwards. It was striking and powerful, and it sent an electric shock thru the audience. I could feel it physically, a wave of energy hitting my chest. Some people near me whispered excitedly, "It's starting. . . it's starting!"

Kathryn Kuhlman said, in a very strong voice, that there were three men in the balcony, to her right, that had had back trouble, and were now healed. "The one with the brace can take it off". . . Then it was somebody in the back with severe asthma. . . then somebody on the main floor with something. . . then it started happening all over. There was an incredible, indescribable energy and presence in that room — it showed me that faith healing is just as real as any other form of healing. I saw many people actually get out of their wheelchairs, healed, walking around joyfully, tearfully, going onto the stage — people who had been paralyzed, people with all kinds of diseases, including polio and multiple sclerosis. . . They would come on the stage to thank her, and she would say, "Don't thank me, *I* didn't do it. . ." One man had had multiple sclerosis for 20 years, and he was cured. "I *shot* out of that wheelchair," he said, with tears, and with beautiful enthusiasm, "some strong force just threw me right out of it. . ." Joy was rampant.

a good meditation . . . a healing experience

I doubt that any of it was faked. Even if some of it was, as skeptics want to believe, the effect of it all was wonderful. People were radiant and joyful as they left. . . I felt strangely light and calm: it was a good meditation. . . it was a healing experience for all of us in that auditorium.

A few years after that Katherine Kuhlman passed on, into a higher, lighter body. She was a great healer — I've felt grateful that I had the experience of seeing her, and feeling the energy that she could channel. . .

Going home

I WENT BACK TO MINNESOTA — it seemed to have changed a great deal, becoming much more open and accepting. . . Then I realized that *I* had changed a great deal — I was much more open and accepting. . .

Back to Minnesota

I saw my folks for the first time in years, and spent nearly the whole summer with them. I was looking at them with new eyes — I was impressed, deeply touched by their humor, their capabilities, their love for each other, their love of life. I felt very warm and welcome — it was good to come back home.

We had a beautiful talk one night before I left. . . I found myself saying I loved them — something I don't think I've ever done, unless as a little kid. . . It seemed as if they had changed so much, and they had actually. We all had. The whole country had. The war was over.

the war was over

Yet, I saw that the deepest changes had taken place within me. . . I was no longer rejecting my parents, my culture, my roots — I was seeing it all in a new light. . . and it was all because I was no longer rejecting myself — my past, my choices, my path. . . I saw change everywhere. . .

My folks had gotten into organic gardening, and were spending a lot of time up north, in their cabin on a pine-surrounded lake, without a phone or TV. . . And big trees had grown all around their home, and for the first time, I saw that Suburbia has the potential to become a beautiful, open forest, as more and more open people live there. . .

hope for Suburbia

I roamed around my old neighborhood, full of memories. . .

I went up north at the end of the summer and went ricing with old friends — gathering wild rice from the shallow lakes, poling thru in canoes. . .

141

Magic

Western magic

I MET PEOPLE up there in the north country who were good friends of my brother's, and who were into the Western esoteric tradition of ritual magic. We spent many hours talking, comparing, contrasting. . . The teachings are very similar to those I had been studying at the Tibetan Center. It was so good to find teachings and practices in the West as brilliant as those in the East. Since then, I have found many, many of them, both exoteric, or outer — such as the Science of Mind Church, and Catherine Ponder's *Pray and Grow Rich* — and esoteric, or inner — such as Israel Regardie's writings, especially *The Art of True Healing*.

outer & inner

The biggest difficulty in the comprehension of Eastern teachings, I had come to feel, is their translation into a foreign language and culture. The teachings coming from the West don't have this culture shock and language gap.

It was before that summer, while still with Carol, that I had discovered the teachings of the Essenes and the Gnostics — deep, beautiful teachings which had, unfortunately, been edited out of the accepted Christian literature in the conservative takeover of the 4th century AD.

ancient teachings re-emerging

The recent discovery of the Essene and Gnostic library now commonly known as the Dead Sea scrolls is no accident — it is but yet another sign that more and more ancient teachings are re-emerging once again, as more and more people are evolving into a level of consciousness which can comprehend those teachings.

What exactly is magic? There are many, many different forms of magic. Basically — in essence — we are all magical creations... the Universe is a magic show...

An attempted definition of magic

Some physicist recently said that the nature of reality can best be compared to a hologram, a three-dimensional image which gives our eyes all the information for us to perceive a solid, material object there, and yet, it is empty space, devoid of any object. A hologram is magic. The nature of the Universe is magical. God is a magician...

Magic has many definitions. Webster defines it abominably. (Don't bother looking it up.) One attempted definition: Magic is awareness of, and use of, a higher reality beyond that which we perceive thru our physical senses. This higher reality includes *causal* planes, planes which can cause changes to manifest on a physical plane. Before we build a house, we must have a blueprint. By creating the house first in our imaginary mental vision, and then on paper in a blueprint, and finally in physical form, we are accomplishing a magical process. Life itself is a magical process.

I once saw, on a very special occasion, the three highest lamas of the Nyingma school of Tibetan Buddhism touring Dharma Press in Emeryville, California. They stared in wonder and amazement as a young western student showed them a Harris TXT Photocomposition typesetting computer, which has a memory which operates based on increments of a millionth of a second (or microseconds), and which can photograph 40 individual letters per second from discs which whirl around 2400 times a minute...

everything is magic

Dudjom Rinpoche, head of the Nyingmas, turned to the others and said, "This is magic . . . this is magic!"

Everything is magic. You might as well enjoy the show...

Living Love

Joining the staff of the Living Love Center

IN THE FALL, I went back to the Living Love Center in Berkeley, and joined the staff, working with a wild, innovative Aquarius actress named Collin Wilcox, and an amazing, totally unique and beautiful songwriter named Summer Raven. The three of us were 'The Player's Department," and it was our work (our 'karma yoga', as we all called our work) to write and perform music and skits, for the trainings, and for the house in general. . . It was one of the most beautiful 'jobs' I've ever encountered: room, board, and a small salary just for writing and playing music and acting and growing and having a good time.

The Living Love Center was so wide open in so many different ways, at that time. . .

I had never seen a large group living in such harmony

They were such new-age innovators, trying so many new techniques — some original, some from a wide variety of different sources. . . Every person there had something to contribute. . . And I had never seen such a large group living in such harmony. Living there proved to me that a group can live together with a very close and easy rapport, just by applying a few principles, and practicing a few simple group techniques or rituals. . .

sharing undelivered communications

The most important thing is *sharing* with each other, in some form. Undelivered communications — especially those of a so-called 'negative' or 'separating' nature — must be accepted and communicated, otherwise they fester and expand and lead to all kinds of difficulties.

OM

One night a week, every one who lived in the house would gather, form a circle, and chant OM together for a minute or so. . . The whole group would immediately quiet, center, focus, relax, and come together during and after this simple chant. The OM was often followed by a few minutes of silence — moments I cherished. Then, one person would sit in the center of the circle, and everyone in the circle would, in their turn, give them any 'undelivered communications', usually beginning with words such as "I

make myself feel separate from you when you
_____" — or something similar. . .

It is a difficult process, demanding honesty. . . But it leaves the air feeling very cleansed afterwards, and it brings the whole family very close together. . . Communication is a key to group communion, the essence of community. . .

communication, communion, community

One night, we reversed the process and had the people tell each other what they *liked* about each other. It was fantastic. . . there was so much love in that room — love which is rarely communicated so openly. . .

Another of the most effective practices the group did, I felt, was to go around the circle each week, and have everyone choose their own *sadhana*, or special, personal discipline or practice, for the week. . . It was understood that everyone was there for their growth, and people knew in their hearts the best paths for themselves. . .

Once again, just as in our community in Oregon, I had found a place where people were encouraged to do what they felt best about. . . Free will was encouraged, and respected.

I met a beautiful lady named Shakti Gawain while at the Living Love Center. She is a dancer, tall and lithe, full of energy. . . She had just returned from a two-year journey around the world, having spent most of her time in Italy and then India. . . We soon became friends, and we soon became lovers. . . (When I first read this manuscript to Shakti, she said, "You should say, 'We soon became lovers, and then we became friends.' ")

a beautiful lady

There was a relaxed closeness between us from the first, as if we were old friends. . . And that feeling is always there. . . But the beginning of our relationship was in some ways marred by some demands I was making upon her, which I wasn't even aware of until much later:

For many, many months after my first weekend Intensive at the Living Love Center, I felt no jealousy or anger or fear, that I was aware of. . . Part of it was the high from the intensity of the weekend experience, and the daily life, at the Center. . . and part of it reflected deep, evolutionary change that had taken place within me. . . Yet part of it, too, was that I had cut myself off from recognizing my own feelings of a negative or separating nature — and in doing

falling for a trap

so, I had cut myself off from others, and I found it very difficult to relate to people's problems and anger and fears. . .

And I fell for a trap: I thought that, because I felt I had overcome fear and anger and jealousy, others should do so too. . . I became unaccepting, even critical of others, in many ways. . .

I was especially hard on Shakti, without even being aware of it, telling her she shouldn't feel jealous, or fearful, or angry, or whatever. . . I felt I had left those unnecessary emotions behind — why couldn't she?

It took me a year to see that I was laying some very intense models of behavior on Shakti, and others — heavy demands of how they should be acting. . . And it took me almost a year before I found myself experiencing some jealousy again, and anger, and fear. When I did, it even felt good — it felt warm and natural. . . it felt like I had rejoined the human race.

I had learned so much. . . yet, I still have so much more to learn. . . Evolution is an endless process — if any person in a human body feels they have nothing more to learn, or nowhere to grow, I feel they are being misled. . .

one step closer to Utopia

My friend Kent and I drove up to Eugene, Oregon for a weekend, to see Barbara Neill. . . At one point I said that I had almost discovered how to create a Utopia, except for the problem of jealousy. . .

And Kent said, "Why not just accept jealousy?"

I must have been ready to hear those words, because I really heard those words. . . They blew me away. . . and I became one step closer to Utopia. . .

my new family

When I first came to the Living Love Center, it was so open, so loose — it was creative anarchy. And an amazingly creative group of people were drawn to it — a group of artists and musicians and builders and poets and dancers and teachers and lovers that has remained connected ever since. But then Ken Keyes, the director, in his own quiet but very strong way, started controlling things more rigidly. He is a Capricorn, after all, and things had gotten so Aquarian they were nearly out of his control. . .

resistance

I started to feel that Ken had written a book which was brilliantly channeled, for the most part, in the heights of open, inspired breakthrus into higher consciousness. . . But then, on a day-to-day level, he has had difficulty interpreting and understanding his own teachings in the book. . . Not that I mean to criticize him — he has done a lot of good for a lot of people — including me. He is serving humanity in a beautiful way — he is spreading light and love. . . Yet I began to feel that he is interpreting his own teachings in a narrow, limited fashion.

He initiated a '90-day program' which was heavily regimented, heavily scheduled, and filled with restrictive rules, in spite of nearly every staff member's protest. . . Most of the staff was required to participate. . . There was much resistance. I felt that Ken was much more effective as a teacher while he was doing weekends, and when he let people have more freedom and individual choice. . . But he felt a need to focus, to tighten things up, and I respected his choice.

Yet I felt I wouldn't stay there too much longer.

There is a season for everything — a time to join a group, and a time to leave. . . a time for discipline, and a time to relax. . . As things became more and more disciplined around the Center, I started to relax more and more. I had had several years of discipline, and I was ready for a change.

a season for everything

Leaving the Center happened quite smoothly and organically. A group of us went off into the mountains south of San Francisco to record an album of our music. (By 'coincidence', it happened to be on the same piece of land that the Floating Lotus had lived on!)

a band, an album. . .

When we came back to the Center, the band had grown, and the Center had grown, and there wasn't enough space for all of us. . . So we found a large house, in North Berkeley, to live in and rehearse in, to prepare for another album.

Suddenly, we were on our own. . . and there were infinite possibilities! Once again, creative anarchy reigned.

and a new home

147

Silva Mind Control

Deep, valuable teachings: everyone is creative . . . everyone is psychic

I ENCOUNTERED ANOTHER SET OF TEACHINGS at this time, which has proved very useful.

I took a course called Silva Mind Control, and read a book called *Psychic Development* by Jean Porter. They confirmed something I was beginning to feel: *everyone* is naturally creative, and even a natural psychic — all we need to do is to learn to relax, and tune into our own feelings (the key to our intuition), and trust ourselves, and use our senses in a more spontaneous way. . .

the birth of Silva Mind Control

The story I heard is that Jose Silva, a Mexican-American living in Laredo, Texas, started it all by teaching his kids little psychic tricks to use in school. Before each class, he told them to just relax for a moment, take a deep breath, close their eyes, and give themselves a positive autosuggestion such as, "I am going to effortlessly absorb everything I need in this class. . ." And before each test he'd have them relax for a moment and tell themselves, "I'm going to do very well in this test. . . Whatever answers I need will easily come to mind. . ."

His children did very well in school — and soon he was teaching many of the neighbor kids the same techniques. . .

developing psychic potential

Those kids grew up, naturally and easily developing their psychic potential.

Silva began to dream of setting up an Institute to teach psychic awareness, or magic, or 'mind control', as he likes to call it. But that would take capital — about $10,000, he figured.

One night, he had a dream, in which he saw a big number of several digits, very clearly. The next day, his wife asked him to drive to Mexico to get something in a grocery store. In the store, he saw a lottery ticket with the same number on it that he had seen in his dream. . . He bought the ticket, and won the lottery — which was worth $10,000. . . So he was able to set up his Institute, and start teaching. Many of his kids and the neighbors, now grown up, and now highly developed psychics, joined him as his staff. . .

The Mind Control classes are pure magic, in a beautifully clear and simple form. . . They present a great deal of information, based on scientific research. And they take you repeatedly into a very relaxed state, a state of alpha brain wave activity. . . There's nothing mysterious about it, actually: just relax. . . Just take a deep breath, and relax your body, then take another deep breath and relax your mind, and then take a third deep breath and let go completely. . . Count down from ten to one if you wish to deepen the relaxation, going deeper with each count. . . Repeat the whole process if you wish to deepen further. . . Now your brain is at an alpha brain wave level. . .

classes in magic

Once you are in this relaxed state, there are all kinds of possibilities. . .

You can aid your body in healing itself, just by mentally sending healing energy. . . You can recreate your body. . . You can tune into your own natural genius. . . You can do creative visualization. . . You can picture yourself easily accomplishing whatever it is you dream of doing — and by doing so repeatedly, you can make it a reality. . . You can seek and meet spirit guides, or 'imaginary' counselors, or guardian angels, who can assist you in anything, everything. . .

You can help and even heal others, even at a distance, with the powers of your mind, just by relaxing, and sending them healing energy, and visualizing their bodies being cleansed, healed. . . Thoughts have wings — and thoughts are *things*, just as substantial (and as insubstantial) as anything else. Through our thoughts, we create our world.

Many things I learned while taking Silva Mind Control have been with me ever since. . . I remember my dreams simply by saying to myself, as I lie down in bed and relax, "I will remember my dreams. . . and their meaning will be clear to me." I send myself and my friends healing energy — and I have seen and felt its good effects.

my spirit guides   And I have met two spirit guides, who are always with me, whenever I call. . . One is named Mu, and he is beautiful, always changing, with a wild sense of humor. . . Sometimes, when I'm very active, he tells me to shut up and sit down and listen to him. . . The other is named Sara (rhymes with Tara). . . She rarely says anything, but she sings sweet melodies and plays stringed instruments. I think she is the force behind the music and poetry I have written, because, after meeting her, it began to flow on its own energy, with no conscious summoning or control on my part. . . Music, poetry, and other writing of assorted types started to burst forth, at odd moments, in dreams, in coffee houses, in the middle of conversations, even making love. . .

the Muses live   The Muses live. . . Each one of us can find our own in our own way. . .

Relationship

a lover and a teacher   SHAKTI BECAME a beautiful lover, and a beautiful teacher for me. We both have things to teach each other, and we both have things to learn from each other — a healthy, growing basis for a relationship. . .

I'm seeing now that one of the finest opportunities for growth is within relationship with other people. . . Be honest with each other — confront your problems openly: your relationships are a mirror of your mind, a mandala, a meditation in action. And, even though usually unconsciously, we always choose relationships which have something very important to teach us. . .

truly tantric   Shakti delights in explorations of emotions — that is her key. . . she is truly tantric, in her own unique way.

If I feel myself separate from someone, having difficulties with someone, my natural inclination is to go within myself, to look at the situation, and to resolve it by seeing it for what it is, and by letting go of any resistance I have toward that person, and by sending them (and myself) blessings — positive, accepting thoughts. . . I've found that this can work miracles. . .

Shakti's natural way is to go directly to that person and to say, "Hey, I'm feeling separate from you. . ." or "I'm angry" or "I'm hurt" or whatever the emotion is. . . She puts out her feelings, her experience, openly to the other person. . . And in doing so, an amazing thing happens: the hard feelings dissolve. . . the darkness of the separation disappears in the light of open investigation and acceptance.

Now, after being together, I'm learning Shakti's method, and she's learning mine. It is good to know both. . . Sometimes one of them proves much more effective than the other. . .

Shakti has become more and more beautiful. . . she is a Libra, after all, which is ruled by Venus, and she has grown more and more, naturally developing the qualities associated with Venus: love, harmony, acceptance. . . a very unique genius is shining thru her — as it is thru everyone else, if we see it. . .

Thanks to Shakti, and thanks to a teacher in Marin County named Kaskafayet, I have learned much more about anger and the other so-called 'negative' emotions. Shakti kept pointing out that I was rejecting anger, in myself and others — I was afraid of my anger, in a way I couldn't see. And that was why I was not dealing with it effectively, at times, and that was why I was rejecting anger in others.

Shakti's words seemed very clear to me. I couldn't deny them. She said I had been confusing anger with *violence*. . . I was deeply aware that violence only leads to more violence, and so it is something to be avoided, or better yet, transmuted. Yet anger is not violence. Violence only occurs after anger has been deeply and repeatedly repressed, and builds in intensity, becoming distorted and harmful. Anger, in itself, is a natural and even useful emotion, and it is usually

effective methods

Shakti and Kaskafayet:

anger is not violence

anger: natural and useful

based upon a clear perception of how someone is limiting themselves, holding themselves back, keeping them from manifesting in a strong, capable, positive way. . .

Kaskafayet

Shakti took a two-weekend intensive at a place called the Kaskafayet Foundation in Marin County, north of San Francisco (the foundation is now called WorldWorks). . . She came back radiant, transformed, eyes shining brightly. . . She said that much of the intensive had focused on learning to trust our own feelings and experience, rejecting none of it, including anger. In fact, much of the power of the course came from looking at anger in a totally new way.

everyone is truly magnificent

The basic premise which Kaskafayet puts forth is that everyone is truly a magnificent being — expansive, creative, and free — but we try to hide our greatness, our own natural genius, and our own emotions because we mistakenly believe that others can't handle it. We aren't giving others credit for being strong enough to take our honest feedback and the full expression of our natural creativity.

we really love one another

We are all very perceptive — we are all intuitive beings. We *know* when other people are holding themselves back, limiting themselves. And this is often the source of our anger: we get angry with people because we see how they are making themselves smaller, weaker, than they actually are. And we really love one another, in our hearts. And anger is an expression of that love. Look at Christ when he threw the money changers out of the Temple — there was anger, and there was love. . .

152

I've come to see and to believe that everyone is a genius — and everyone is a fool. It's not a matter of being one or the other, or of being somewhere in between the two. We are both. Everyone has an enlightened genius within them — perceptive, creative, intelligent, powerful. It's all just a matter of seeing who we really are, and letting ourselves have the space to express ourselves. . .

You are a genius

> *I give to you*
>   *the best gift there can be —*
> *I give you a mirror*
>   *and now you can see*
> *The wonder you are!*
>   *To see it is to be free*
> *Look in the mirror now —*
>   *Miracles unfold in front of thee*

Making Love

MANY OF THE DEEPEST TEACHINGS I have received have come while making love. At first the things I learned in loving were painful and difficult, but they have become progressively brighter, clearer, more wondrous. . .

The first time I made love

The first time I made love was in my first year of college. I was drunk, she was drunk, it was rapid and casual, and I felt terrible afterwards. And yet, there was something exquisite in it, though it seemed deeply buried. . .

Over the years I have been blessed with many deep relationships, and I have come to see that every one of them has a purpose, and everyone has something to share with me and to teach me.

My feelings about the sexual act have changed dramatically — like so many other things in my life. At first it was scary, unknown, dark, somewhat magical, but shrouded in guilt and doubt and fears of many nameless and shapeless forms.

Then it became enjoyable. . .

Then, as I grew to know and love Carol, and some others who are very special, like Barbara Neill, making love became something deeply enjoyable, satisfying physically, emotionally, and spiritually, a way of sharing joy and light. . . something I treasured. . .

and then it became sacred

And then, as I grew close to Shakti — and a few others, too, including a radiant being named Star — making love took on much deeper dimensions. Making love is a sacred ritual. It is the act of creation. Our bodies are temples, and when two bodies are joined, we enter into each other's temple. It is a chance to unite with a person's highest self, if we see it that way. . . It is an opportunity to realize that we are, in our deepest levels of being, divine and free, filled with light and love to share with others.

One golden sunlit morning, Shakti and I were making love in a room filled with plants and windows and light. As I watched the light dance on her exquisite body, I realized that, by making love, I was being blessed with a vision of the divine.

Words started pouring thru my consciousness, so clearly and insistently that I had to stop and write them down. . . Then we went back to making love. . . then more words would pour forth and I would lean over and scribble them down. . .

Two hours later, as we were lying very quietly, a very special poem was finished, called:

a very special poem

Making Love

I remember every lover
　with such sweet feelings
I dream of divine dakinis*
　with such sweet prayer
Every woman is a blessing —
　God's creation
Every body is a miracle —
　the Mind's revelation

Every moment of love —
　Sweet inspiration!
Every one is Divine
　as they open to their depths
Such exquisite ritual
　Sweet meditation!
The forces of creation
　unfolding within us
The Kingdom of Heaven
　is truly within us

---

* 'Dakinis' are the angels of Tibet and India. They bring teachings and light. Every woman is a dakini.

Remember the myths
    from our deep past heritage —
Leda and the Swam. . .
    Europa and the Bull. . .
The form of God appearing
    in a shower of gold
To a woman of exquisite
    divine earthly beauty!

In love are all the teachings —
    the deep truths of tantra
In love are all the forces
    of the Universe on display
For all to see, to catch,
    to understand
And to enjoy the Bliss
    of Union of the Divine

Within every woman —
    the forces of the Moon
Within every man —
    the forces of the Sun
Moon unites with the Sun
    eclipsing into One
And a New Moon is born,
    a new light is born!
        And we are reborn,
            continuously reborn

Within every woman —
    the forces of the Earth
Within every man —
    the forces of the Skies
Earth and Sky unite
    and Heaven is here!
Totally illumined,
    if we but understand it
Totally blissed
    with Vision Divine

If the Universe provides
 you with a lover,
Make love! Enjoy!
 Unite with the Divine
And if the Universe shows you
 you're to be alone,
Reflect! Enjoy!
 Unite with the Divine

 —for—

The greatest blessing
 of all in love is that
It's always ever
 within us
We're man and woman
 old and young
The union is ever
 within us

So
 We don't have to hold on
  to anyone else
 We don't need a lover
  to be in love
 God takes care
  of all His creatures
 Even alone,
  we're never alone
 Mother Nature takes care
  of all Her creatures
 Even alone,
  we're always all one

Now...

I LIVED FOR AWHILE in a vacant, abandoned house — the owner had wanted someone there to try to prevent vandalism. Someone had spray painted every wall with huge letters and intense colors that read

a message from a prophet

Now!

At one point, I suddenly realized those words had a clear, loud message for me: Every moment should be lived as fully and as deeply as possible — now... After all, that's all there is. The past is dead, the future is yet to be born...

I think I know who spray painted that word. He's a prophet in rags.

Now...

My story is coming to an end, and I wish to leave you with these thoughts:

Thruout our history we see recurring patterns, in which thought forms, governments, art forms, religions, lifestyles, philosophies, even sciences like medicine, etc, become meaningful and accepted and popular, and then become established and powerful, and then become corrupt and stagnant, losing the vision of their birth, then decaying and dying as new seeds of new forms of life and light are born... Over and over, the light becomes dark, and the dark becomes light...

We are now collectively emerging into a new light, a new consciousness.

Something magical is being reborn among the people...

Something very magical is being reborn among the people, something with many new and ancient forms, seen and felt in the streets and parks and country, in music and festivals, classes and gatherings, in the recent developments of scientific research, in the spiritual energies so evident on the West Coast, and in so many other places...

a global-wide transformation

We are beginning to experience a global-wide transformation, where people are attaining a level of consciousness in which they are, once again, sensitive to each other and to the planet itself... Every person has human rights, and our planet has planetary rights — the right to be treated with love and respect and thankfulness... the right to have clean rivers and oceans and pure air and forests and even wild places where people cannot go, where nature's magic can blossom...

Now...

A new age of light is born

A new age is dawning... It is true — for those who have eyes to see... an age that many have called the Aquarian Age... It is here and now...

This is a time of multi-dimensional information explosions... mass leaps of consciousness... It's a time when a huge number, an infinite number, of different trips emerge — different paths, different possibilities, different choices, from computers to covens...

The wisdom of the ancient traditions once again is being taught and understood, once again being reborn among the people... The American Indian teachings are re-emerging once again — the Phoenix rises! Tibet, too, is being re-born in America... and the spirit of Mother India has come to many parts of the West...

The West is becoming Easternized just as fast as the East is becoming Westernized — fortunately. . . A balance is once more being restored — one which will heal this planet. . .

A balance is being restored — one which will heal this planet

One of Padma Sambhava's predictions (made roughly 800 AD) is *"When the iron bird flies and horses move on wheels, Tibetans will be scattered like ants across the earth and the Dharma will come to the land of the red man. . ."*
Put it in whatever words you wish — there is an awakening happening in the West. . .

Suddenly, a countless number of spiritual and psychological and scientific paths have emerged and re-emerged which were not available in the streams of mass consciousness 10 years ago. . .

There's 'Trans-personal' psychology — Western science beginning to see and dissolve its limitations. . . There's so many forms of Western mysticism. . . the Essene healers. . . so many natural healers, like Mildred Jackson, and Michael Samuels with his *Well Body Book*. . . so many spiritual healers, like Patricia Sun, Joel Goldsmith, Kathryn Kuhlman. . . so many people from so many different cultures and backgrounds are speaking once more, and being heard. . .

Western science and mysticism

So many communal groups, of so many different types are flourishing. . . the Findhorn community in Scotland is re-discovering elves and spirits of the plants — some of them have seen Pan. . . The Native American Church is strong again, with their deeply sacred rituals. . . The Indian songs for growing and hunting and healing are being remembered. . . The traditions are being restored. . .

communal groups

So many people are having psychic openings, and becoming aware of new realities which were previously unavailable, and discovering teachings that are deeply meaningful and beautiful and healing. . . Jane Roberts and Seth. . . Kaskafayet. . . Jim Hurtak and Janice Cohen. . . Uri Geller. . . Edgar Mitchell. . . J.R.R. Tolkien. . . Ursala K. LeGuin. . . Einstein. . . John Lilly. . .

psychic openings

161

The second coming of Christ...

The Aquarian Gospel of Jesus the Christ has been written... This and many other sources are proclaiming that we are entering into a new age, one which rediscovers the inner meanings of the teachings of Christ... Some believe the second coming of Christ is imminent... and many deeply feel that He has come already — as a spirit which is within all of us, here and now, if it is but seen and understood.

teachings widely published...

The teachings of many orders and sources are being widely published... Tarot is once again being used meaningfully and respectfully... A whole new Astrology is emerging, one which is uplifting and clarifying — a powerful tool for growth and change...

magic and witchcraft and meditation:

Magic in many, many forms is being practiced... Witches are meeting in covens again, and are growing deeply, and healing, and spreading light... Meditation groups of countless forms and practices are blossoming...

And Maharishi Mahesh Yogi is even proclaiming that, if just one percent of the country's population meditates, the result will be to uplevel the mass consciousness enough so that crime will be substantially reduced in the cities, and international tensions will decrease... And we will have a Paradise on Earth...

a Paradise on Earth

And so many groups and gurus and individuals and couples and families are moving to the country... There are a vast number of loosely connected spiritual, psychological, ecological, artistic, and *whatever* groups that have a network of new age land holdings across the world...

And there are countless groups and trips that I've never even heard of... There are many, many systems, techniques, sciences, fields of research, forms of ecological living, meditations, etc, *etc,* that you're aware of and that I am not aware of...

There are infinite paths — and they all lead up the same mountain, the mountain of human evolution...

A new kind of acceptance is being born which is very healthy: a *live and let live* attitude. . . More and more deviation from the 'norm' (whatever that was) is allowed. . . This is resulting in a true freedom for all people. You are free to do exactly what you wish, in your heart. . . whether you get married, or don't get married. . . have children or not. . . whether you're gay or straight or bi. . . into the city or the country. . . whether you're into magic or music or mathematics or mushrooms. . . TM or TV. . .

You are free to do exactly as you wish. . . as long as you don't infringe on somebody else's freedom. . .

So many aware and open people are becoming doctors, lawyers, teachers, mechanics, politicians, computer programmers, farmers, healers, postal employees, wanderers, home makers, truck drivers, even *police people*, even prisoners, that we are beginning to see vast changes happening organically from *within* the systems. . . And, at the same time, there are totally new lifestyles evolving outside of these systems, which are becoming less and less reliant upon them. . .

This is the beginning of a New Renaissance — happening only for those who have eyes to see, yet very definitely happening.

In many ways my search has come full circle. . . In many ways the vision is becoming manifest. . . Faust's search for knowledge is bearing fruits . . .

I feel as if all the searching I've been thru, and all the teachings I've been given, have finally taken root, and sprouted into the light, and grown. . . And my path has led back home. . . it has led to *me*, to seeing that I have understanding and awareness within my own heart, just as everyone does, if we but see it. . .

Every teacher who is worthy to be called a teacher keeps pointing into the very hearts of his/her students — that is where the answers lie. . . As a great Master put it,

> *The Truth is within you. . .*
> *The Kingdom of Heaven is within you. . .*

A new acceptance

a New Renaissance

my path has led back home

Sometimes we need help unlocking the door... sometimes we need someone else to give us a key... But that key always unlocks something within us...

Everyone is a guru

I have gone from seeking for a guru, to seeing that everyone is a guru — everyone has their thing to express, to teach...

We are all creative beings

We are all creative beings... each of us has our own unique individual creative genius... Let a thousand flowers bloom...

Now...

What's next?
Anything is possible.

I was quietly sitting awhile ago, and words such as these flowed thru my being:

Evolutionary leaps

I have a strong feeling that the violence and rebellion of the 60s (*symbolized by Mars, if you're into astrology*) has changed into a new kind of acceptance and live-and-let-live attitude in the 70s (*symbolized by Venus*)... This openness and respect for human rights — our own as well as others — is preparing the way for vast, even unimagined change in the 80s and 90s (*symbolized by Uranus – the planetary force ruling Aquarius...*), when a great many people will experience deep transformation, and when many 'established' ways of life will fade and many new ways come into being.

We are beginning an evolutionary leap into a greater development than we can even imagine at this time...

Key words which open the gates into this Renaissance are *creative anarchy*... Three more are *Love one another*...

There are infinite possibilities.

A Dream, a Reality...

I HAD A DREAM, not long ago, a vision in a dream, one I remember vividly, shining brightly in my memory... a dream which showed me a deep truth — a dream which showed me the nature of reality...

A dream of reality, filled with promise

I was walking alone, thru rocky country... The land around me was beautiful, but it was hazy, kind of foggy, and there were rocks on the path I was following...

The path rounded a turn, and there was a large gate in front of an opening in a huge rock before me... The gate was completely covered with ornate wrought-iron grillwork... In the center of the grillwork was a tangled mass of wrought-iron, a knot... It looked like a puzzle to me, and I went up to it and reached into it...

I found a handle, and pulled, and into my hand came a sword, with a guard of tangled wrought-iron which covered my hand...

Pulling the sword out opened up the lock, and a door swung open, automatically. I entered, holding the sword in my hand, into a dark cave. It was frightening, yet exciting, too, as if filled with promise.

Soon I saw a golden light filtering thru the dark tunnel ahead. And I entered into a huge, dazzlingly beautiful chamber, with a high, vaulted roof, filled with golden light as if from thousands of candles...

There were three altars in the chamber — one close to the entrance, one midway between the others, and one in the center. I was immediately drawn to them, as if they had a magnetic energy...

Three altars

I went up to the first one, closest to me, nearest the entrance. It was the size of a small dinner table, covered with a white cloth, and it was filled with objects of all kinds: candles, bells, books, pictures, statues, food, water, flowers, incense, even gold and jewels and money.

The first altar: It was packed full of things. As I examined them, these words were clearly transmitted to me: I didn't hear any voice or see anyone — it was more of a telepathic communication, saying:

the physical

"This is the material plane, filled with all the things you can see, touch, hear, taste, and smell. It is a truly beautiful creation. . . none of it needs to be rejected. . . it is yours to work with and play with and enjoy.

The second altar: It felt as if a beautiful gift had been given to me. And then I went on, drawn to the second altar in the middle. It was about the same size, but it was lighter, brighter, of a less dense quality, shimmering, like a vision. It had just a very few things on it — a staff or wand, a cup, a sword, and a pentacle: the suits of the Tarot deck — the instruments of magic. They, too, were shimmering, almost transparent. And these words came to me:

the magical

"This is the astral plane, beyond the physical – the plane where the physical is imagined, and created. This is the plane of magic. It is a truly beautiful creation – none of it needs to be rejected – and it is yours to work with and play with and enjoy. . ."

The third altar: It felt as if another, even more beautiful and wondrous gift had been given to me. . . And then I went on, drawn to the third altar in the very center of the golden temple. There was no sound — it was deeply, profoundly silent. The third altar was the same size as the first two, but it was so light, so shimmering, that it was nearly non-existent. And there was nothing on it at all, nothing but the play of wondrous golden light.

And these words came to me:

the Infinite

"This is the Spiritual plane, beyond the astral, beyond the physical. It is the eternal essence, the seed of all creation. It is truly divine. And it is you, always, in your deepest being. It is all Life. . . It is an endless, wondrous blessing."

And I felt it shower over me, a golden light energy, coming from high above, in the center of the Temple of Light. . . Soon I was in an infinite field of golden, shining light, extending everywhere, eternally. . . The Infinite. . . The seed of creation. . . pure, endless, shining energy — our Essence. . .

I awoke, refreshed, rejuvenated, bathed in joy. I had drunk deeply of the Elixer of Life. I had received a beautiful blessing.

I awoke, into a world filled with infinite possibilities to explore and enjoy. . . feeling free and eternally young. . . and wanting to tell everyone of my dream/vision. . . wanting to say to everyone, from my heart —

a blessing

May you be blessed
with whatever
your heart desires

Appendix

I wrote the following paper for a Psychology course I took one summer at the University of Minnesota, after spending six years studying 'Eastern' psychology. I wish to include it as an appendix in this book, because this paper deals with things which were of central importance to me in my search for understanding, and it reviews much of this book, with a very different perspective...

The instructor's comments are included as sideheads. His words reflect psychology today more accurately than mine... I wasn't ever sure whether he really read the paper or not — like the students, he was far too rushed...

In order to rediscover the ancient roots of our healing and magical traditions, it can be very useful to explore the most modern form of shamanism currently in vogue: Western science.

The 'witch doctors' of today are the psychologists and the medical doctors — that's what the people believe in, and so that is what can cure the people (although these beliefs are rapidly crumbling, witnessed by the growing number of alternative healing forms, and the number of doctors that are being sued for malpractice).

Popular 'yoga' in the West is psychology; psychology, like everything else, is in a period of incredibly rapid growth and change, exploding into a huge number of different forms and techniques. How long will it be before our educational system becomes aware of it?

As an appendix, a paper for a Psychology course

the sideheads which follow are the instructor's comments (not mine!) which were scribbled in the margin of the paper

The study of psychology: East and West

Prologue

A brief look at my personal background may be useful before I present the main ideas of this paper.

I attended the University of Minnesota from 1964-1968, majoring in Theater and English. I took what was called at that time Psychology 1 and 2 — Introduction to Psychology. It was not an impressive course — both the teaching methods and the course content left much to be desired.

169

I began to study yoga and Vedic philosophy in 1967. By that time I was deeply questioning the University's teaching methods and course content and *raison d'etre* in general. I finally left the University, about 12 credits short of graduation, to go to California to study yoga and Eastern thought. Now, six years later, I have returned to finish my undergraduate work; this will be my last undergrad course at the U., if all goes well.

I spent a year studying yoga, two years studying Zen, and three years studying Tibetan Buddhism. My last year was spent working toward a Master's Degree at the Nyingma Institute in Berkeley, a Tibetan Buddhist center with an American form, which can grant graduate degrees.

I gradually became aware during the course of these studies that I was studying *psychology* — in theory and practice — as well as philosophy and religion and other disciplines simultaneously. Eastern thinking is not nearly so compartmentalized as Western. The search for truth, for an understanding of the nature of existence, the study of the nature of mind, is the basis of their science. Recently, in Berkeley, I became aware of Robert Ornstein's very fascinating book, *The Psychology of Consciousness*. The discovery of left and right brain differences is, in my thinking, a brilliant metaphor for describing and comparing Eastern and Western psychological methods.

I have discussed many of the following ideas with many people, including some Western scientists and therapists on the West Coast, students of both Eastern and Western psychology and philosophy, and a well-known and respected Tibetan teacher and leader, Tarthang Tulku Rinpoche, who agrees with many of these ideas.

The study of psychology: East and West

Some random thoughts

I wish to approach this paper, not in the usual way that seems to be (both consciously and unconsciously) required of students in most classes, but rather with a more spontaneous, and hopefully more creative, approach.

That's all simply a matter of personal judgement, of course, but I hope in this paper to be free to offer a collage of thinking coming from a variety of different traditions, different perspectives, different points of view. . .

First I'd like to focus on the recent Western investigations into right and left brain functions, then explore some Eastern psychological teaching methods, and then look at some of the implications of the above for the West.

Left and right brain functions

Recent Western experimental techniques have discovered physiologically what various Eastern traditions have been exploring and describing for literally thousands of years: our thinking processes are only a limited part of our whole mental process; our thinking cannot fully understand the nature of reality, simply because it is beyond thought.

It has been discovered that the cerebral cortex has been divided into two hemispheres (see: R. Ornstein, *The Psychology of Consciousness*). The left hemisphere (in most right-handed people) deals with all verbal, conceptual thinking, logic, mathematics; the right hemisphere, which Ornstein calls the 'holistic' side, involves intuitive, depth understanding of *whole* systems, and it involves color, music, recognition of familiar faces, intuition, and a great deal that has been so far very difficult to study with traditional Western methods.

Jose Arguelles even suggests that left brain neurons and synapses are fused in a linear fashion, like a computer circuit, while right brain structure is not linear at all. Left brain functions can be duplicated by computer, but right brain cannot. Computers can do brilliant mathematical calculations, but they can't recognize handwriting even as well as the average 3rd grader — recognition of handwriting, like recognizing faces, involves some right brain intuitive activity.

Not true. With the proper software we do as good a job of duplicating right as left. Only reason we do not have right duplicated is little economic reason, so little research on problem.

Many people feel these discoveries have vast implications for Western science — especially in psychology and philosophy — and for studies of Eastern traditions as well.

Arguelles says we can view the entire history of Western man — with it's incredible strength and effectiveness and yet it's amazing lack of foresight and insight — as the history of a people who became dominated by left-brain systems of research and thinking, so much that right-brain understanding was cut off. This is the unique neurosis of the West.

We need now to reunite left and right brain functions, in order to become balanced once again. The West is turning to many different forms of yoga. Yoga literally means 'union' (or 'yoking', which is the same root) — and we are searching for a union of left and right brain functions, which is true understanding.

Teaching methods of Eastern psychology

By 'Eastern' I am referring to a vast assemblage of different cultures, techniques, traditions, which includes classical Indian yoga and Vedanta, Southern (or Theravadan) Buddhism, Tibetan and Chinese Buddhism, Taoism, Zen Buddhism, Sufism of the Middle East, and many other traditions. It is my feeling that

American Indian, African, and many early and/or esoteric Western and Christian traditions have a great many similarities to Eastern traditions, especially when viewed in terms of psychology — but that is much too vast and too unexplored to go into at this time.

By 'psychology' I am referring to attempts to 'understand, describe, predict, and influence' not only behavior, but *mind itself* as well. For thousands of years, Buddhist and Hindu and Sufi thinkers have developed tools to scientifically explore the nature of the mind.

Of course, exploring the mind means becoming aware of and exploring (and even, in some sense, *mapping*) both the left and right hemispheres of cerebral cortex activity. Here, of course, many difficulties arise, because the right brain functions are incapable of being understood or described with left-brain *words* and linear concepts. In fact, rampant, continued left-brain activity (which nearly all of us are doing, nearly all the time) dominates and clouds and obscures right-brain intuitive understanding. That's why the emphasis in Eastern research on calming the mind, and stilling the thought processes — or at least slowing them down enough so you can examine them clearly.

What kind of research are you using

Many things happen as a result of this kind of research, which has a great number of names and forms, some of which are called meditation. First, the left brain functions are clearly seen: we see what thoughts are, we see the nearly continual stream of words going through our mind, we see our left brain's strength and restlessness. Then, as we continue — and it often takes guidance (which can be very useful in saving time in this type of study) or much time — we can see the spaces between the thoughts. At first they are very short — instantaneous perhaps. In our usual state of waking consciousness in daily life, they are almost imperceptible. But as we consciously slow down the workings of our mind (sometimes it can feel just like down-shifting into a lower gear), and as we carefully observe, we can definitely see these spaces between thoughts. And as we look into them, it is possible to extend them for longer and longer periods of time. What we are doing with this technique is opening the door to the right brain — realms of color, sound, intuitive understanding, psychic forms and forces which are beyond words, beyond theories, even beyond conceptual thought.

What evidence do you have. Even if first sentence is true, does not mean 2nd sentence is true.

Right brain understanding goes beyond dualism, beyond categories of any kind. And so, Eastern traditions do not have different, compartmentalized sciences. All science attempts to understand reality, and that reality is beyond any particular approach to it.

172

Eastern writings, attempting to use words to go beyond words, are filled with seeming logical contradictions, with paradox. The left brain can never really describe the right.

> Watch without watching for something.
> Look from the invisible at what you cannot grasp.
> To see and yet to see nothing
> Is freedom in and through yourself.
>
> *Tilopa (an Indian yogi, perhaps 10th century)*

Here's an example of Eastern teaching techniques, which I can certainly describe as instruction in psychology. About 30 students went on a weekend retreat in the country with a Tibetan *lama*. ('Lama' means teacher, or 'guru' in Sanskrit, or even 'master' — one ordained to teach by previous lamas in the lineage.) First, we did quite vigorous physical exercises, and then deep breathing exercises — the effect of both was to relax the body and calm the mind considerably. . . 'OK', the lama said, 'Now — what is mind?' . . . he paused for a long time, perhaps a couple of minutes, while everyone looked within themselves . . . 'what is mind?' . . . (a pause again) . . . 'where is mind? . . . does it have a shape? . . . is there a difference between *mind* and *brain*? . . . what is a thought? . . .'

Do we have a psychology of an individual or can it be applied to other people. If so, what other people. These are the type of questions that psychology was trying to answer in 1890. Unfortunately, they could not design tightly controlled experiments that would lead to specific conclusions, so behaviorism took over.

At a later time, he asked us repeatedly "Who are you? . . . Repeat your name to yourself and ask, Who am I?". . . He questioned and questioned, challenging us to think. . .

Eastern methods are definitely pragmatic. They study psychology for a clear and useful reason, which is never lost sight of: understanding the nature of the mind obviously leads to dissolution of personal problems, and then to openness and personal freedom and an ability to help others with their problems, which stem from a limited understanding of the nature of the mind. Personal problems dissolve automatically as one moves toward the state of perfect balance, called enlightenment or awakening, which is peace and insight which passes all (left-brain) understanding.

Here lies a definite, major difference between the psychology of the East and of the West. The East has a strong and constant, brilliantly shining ideal of perfection which to them is obviously the purpose of all their study. The West, in comparison, seems to be — even in spite of their efforts to do otherwise — still trying to make people *normal*, or adjusted to this society. All of this seems very vague; they haven't been able, of course, to define what 'normal' is, and they haven't had any clear ideal to strive toward, no clear understanding of what perfect mental health is.

What is perfection. Ideals as taught in the Bible, Koran or Mein Kamph?

Teaching methods of Western psychology

After several years of studying Eastern disciplines, I am now returning to the University and taking this psychology course. At first, there was a definite, surprising 'culture shock'. So much of the course time was spent in activity that seemed so obviously irrelevant to the study of psychology. The initial focus was on what was expected of the student to achieve a grade. Much of the time was spent assigning *extensive* amounts of reading, considering the length of time of the course, and talking about the tests and the paper which was required, and the grading scale. I had written several papers in my study of Eastern traditions, but never for a grade. And of course there were no tests. I must accept these tests and papers, and even the competition for grades, as a means of study and growth, in some instances — but I wonder if there aren't better methods, especially in the field of psychology, to explore and to grow in understanding. The entire course — so much, in fact, of the entire Western educational process from grade school on — strikes me as an almost totally left-brain experience. Western education far too often puts the teacher, who knows all the information in his left brain, in front of the students, who, it is assumed, know nothing. The instructor then proceeds to communicate his 'knowledge' from his left brain into the students' left brains. This we call education. The idea of having the students discover the answers within themselves is much too often totally neglected.

This completely left-brain educational process leads to a great mass of 'knowledge' (purely left brain activity), but very little 'wisdom' — in-depth understanding which is a balance of left and right brain activity, functioning together.

I fear that, for this class for example (and it's not a bad example — this class is far more interesting, with far more potential for growth than most), most students will barely have time to read the textbook material, study for the tests, and write the paper. That accounts for almost all of the energy expended on this course of study. The methods of introspection, dialogue, questioning, and most importantly, digesting — assimilating on a gut level what is being given — seem sadly neglected. . .

I felt within my first few moments of sitting in class that the view of 'psychology' itself was quite surprisingly limited: psychology is defined as the study of behavior, not mind — because it was simply assumed that mind itself could not be explored scientifically! I feel as if I have been exploring the mind scientifically, and that there are a vast number of tried and true techniques for this type of research.

I have to deeply question most of the course content too — which inevitably means questioning the 'scientific method', as it is

---

Margin notes:

there is, but psychology must function as part of the total university, whose main job appears to be preparing people for jobs.

not necessarily could not, but has not been explained so little to say, except personal philosophy.

currently practiced, as well. Certainly it is useful, but isn't it limited to left-brain conceptual manipulation of external phenomena?

Many questions which strike me deeply have to do with deep, underlying values and assumptions. . . Shouldn't we examine the limits of the scientific method? Can it really explain reality? Even behavior? Isn't the scientific method, always proceeding from a logical hypothesis, an attempt of the left brain to describe a reality which is beyond itself, forever out of reach? Isn't reality beyond words? Don't we need additional, different attempts and techniques to 'understand, describe, predict, and influence' it?

One short example that comes to mind is the study of dreams. Kalish says (*The Psychology of Human Behavior*, p 111) "Modern technology has been effectively utilized in studying this ancient mystery." And then he goes on to present research results showing us how many times each night we dream, and what happens if our dreaming is interrupted, and finally suggests that dreams can be a means of working out personal problems. Modern technology has been useful in establishing (left brain) data, but it has not even touched on (right-brain) intuitive meaning.

I will venture to say that Western psychology is at a point where it must grow into more holistic views of people. It must take a broader view. And it has a lot to learn from ancient Eastern research.

I don't feel the Eastern systems reject the findings of the Western; I do feel however that in many cases, in many areas, they go far beyond it.

is there something inherently wrong with left-brain concepts.
take philosophy of psychology course taught by Prof. Meehl. Relates directly to that question.
Yes, but what.

There's no conclusion, really

I agree with Robert Ornstein, as reported in *Time Magazine* (July 8, 1974, p 76): "Western man's step-by-step, linear, analytic mode of knowledge has enriched him, but has also impoverished him by draining out, or (driving) underground, his intuition and more holistic ways of perceiving. What Ornstein is after is 'a confluence' of the two streams of knowledge — the techniques of the lab joined to the equally valid but vastly different concerns of mystics like the Sufis. . . Thus, Ornstein is testing one of his theses: that the practices of ancient esoteric traditions, like the development of intuition, can be enhanced by modern technology. We should not, he warns, be limited by what we believe is possible."

The left brain is a fantastically brilliant development, a highly useful tool — but a very poor, weak-sighted master. Left-brain knowledge must be balanced by right-brain understanding.

There's no conclusion, really, to this paper. The comparison of East and West, and of left and right brain functions, has just begun, because it has vast implications that deserve further exploration and experimentation.

Afterword

I am ending with this mantra — a very effective psychological device — and its translation . . . mostly just for the fun of it — it's probably never been included in a psychology student's paper. . .

I would bet it has been

OM MANI PADME HUM

Hail to the jewel of bliss
in the lotus of consciousness!

Good paper. But your argument for right-brain seems to be that left is "bad" or something and right is better. Wouldn't a better method be to point out how we know all this stuff about left and it is great, now lets work on the right and have the two equalize. Our knowledge of

(*The instructor's comments stopped here, somewhat abruptly. . .*)

176

Suggested Reading

Reunion — Tools for Transformation by Mark Allen, Shakti Gawain, and Jon Bernoff (Whatever Publishing*). This book presents many of the most direct, effective, and most easily communicated teachings and *practices* which the authors have absorbed over the years. Part I: Opening; Part II: Understanding; Part III: Tools for transformation; Part IV: Now we're free!

The Art of True Healing by Israel Regardie (originally, Helios Books, England; now, Weiser). Western magic in a nutshell. Powerful theory and techniques in only 42 pages. This is one of the finest works on true magic ever written.

Seven Arrows by Hyemeyohsts Storm (Harper & Row). The American Indian traditions are alive and well, and many teachers are emerging, and remembering. This has beautiful stories, and deep teachings. You learn of the medicine wheel, which is the *mandala*. A very valuable book.

The Nature of Personal Reality by Jane Roberts (Prentice-Hall). One of the Seth books. An incredible view of ourselves and how we truly create our own reality. If you don't have time to deeply read it, at least read part of it — at least the last chapter.

Handbook to Higher Consciousness by Ken Keyes, Jr. (Living Love Publications). One of the clearest expressions of the wisdom of the East in modern relevant terms. Deeply worthwhile.

The Way of Life (or **Tao Te Ching**) by Lao Tzu. The translation by Gia-Fu Feng and Jane English (Vintage) is especially excellent. This book is the basis of Taoism — short, simple, profound poems, with much water imagery, teaching us to go with the flow. Exquisite words.

Lazy Man's Guide to Enlightenment by Thaddeus Golas (Seed Center). Simple, clear, unique.

Pray and Grow Rich by Catherine Ponder (Parker Publishing Co.). A Western meditation manual. One of the best books on affirmation available. Other books by Rev. Ponder are also excellent: **The Healing Secret of the Ages, The Prospering Power of Love** and **The Dynamic Laws of Prosperity**. The author is a minister of the Unity Church, and that church, like Science of Mind, is into all kinds of good things.

2150 by Thea Alexander (Macro Books). A look at a Utopia of the future. Enjoyable reading, deep content — and it could all be true.

Seth Speaks by Jane Roberts (Bantam). A beautiful, clear view of ourselves, and how we truly create our own reality.

Be Here Now (Harmony) and **The Only Dance There Is** (Doubleday) by Ram Dass. He is beautifully, clearly expressive.

The Psychology of Consciousness by Robert Ornstein (Harcourt Brace). The Western scientific mind finally meets the Eastern mystical experience. The result sheds incredible light on both.

Toward the One by Pir Vilayat Khan (Harper & Row). A beautiful, rich book from a Sufi master, filled with practices as well as theory, aimed at uniting all different philosophies and religions.

Autobiography of a Yogi by Yogananda (Wehman). A classic.

The Teachings of Don Juan and **Journey to Ixtlan** and **Tales of Power** and the rest by Carlos Castaneda. New classics.

This is It or **The Book** or any of several others by Alan Watts. He is a genius at translating the wisdom of the East into words understood in the West. Watts wrote **The Way of Zen** when he was only 19 years old, and it remains probably the most brilliant comprehension of the Zen experience by a Westerner that I know of.

The Aquarian Gospel of Jesus the Christ by Levi (De Vorss). A true Western mystic, writing in the last century, revealing a deeper meaning in Christ's teachings that only now — in the dawn of the Aquarian Age — are we ready to receive.

Cutting Through Spiritual Materialism and **Meditation in Action** by Chogyam Trungpa, Rinpoche. Jewels of clear thinking.

Time, Space and Knowledge and **Gesture of Balance** by Tarthang Tulku, Rinpoche (Dharma Press). Destined to be one of the major contributors of ancient Tibetan knowledge to the West.

The Mystic Path to Cosmic Power by Vernon Howard. Very commercial format, but very useful information.

The Art of Spiritual Healing and **Living Now** (Citadel) and any of several others by Joel Goldsmith. The essence of spiritual healing, by a well-known healer.

The Findhorn Garden by the Findhorn community. An exquisitely beautiful book, by a group in Scotland which is re-discovering so much, including nature spirits and devas. . .

The Prophet and **The Forerunner** by Kahlil Gibran. Written by a prophet and a forerunner. Very beautiful. The short story "God's Fool," which opens *The Forerunner* is especially brilliant. Gibran writes for all time.

Psychic Development by Jean Porter. A how-to book. Simple and clear.

The Silva Mind Control Method by Jose Silva (Simon and Schuster). An introduction to magic.

Black Elk Speaks by Niehart. Destined to be a classic.

The Well Body Book by Michael Samuels and Hal Bennett. A holistic approach to health — wonderful and useful, too. The second chapter presents a clear, effective meditation for meeting your spirit guide(s), or counselors, or 'imaginary doctors', or whatever you wish to call them.

The Handbook of Alternatives to Chemical Medicine by Mildred Jackson, N.D., and Terri Teague (Lawton-Teague Publications). Mildred Jackson remembers all the healing techniques our grandmothers knew and our mothers forgot. . . And she knows much, much more. Mildred is a brilliant healer, and her book reflects her vast knowledge. One of her deepest teachings is that *there is no disease which cannot be healed*.

Dawn Visions by Daniel Moore (City Lights Books). Beautiful visionary poetry.

The Gypsies by Jan Yoors (Simon and Schuster). An authentic portrait of the gypsies in Europe written by a German who lived with them for 10 years, from age 12 to 22. The gypsies are mystics and masters, with deep teachings which they pass on in very practical ways.

Astrology for the New Age — An Intuitive Approach by Mark Allen (Whatever Publishing*). A complete course in an ancient science/artform for a new age.

Utopia Here & Now by Mark Allen (Whatever Publishing*). A pamphlet. Why not create a Utopia here and now?

Also. . .

Music by Mark Allen:

Seeds (Whatever Publishing*). A cassette, soon to be out on an album. Hymns for a new age.

Eveningsong (Whatever Publishing*). A album-length cassette. Love songs for a new age.

---

*If it's not in your bookstore, write Whatever Publishing, 722 Alcatraz Ave., no. 204, Oakland, CA 94609.

Be in peace. . .